Praise for *The Talent Manifesto*

"RJ Heckman's brilliant book, *The Talent Manifesto*, challenges conventional notions of talent management: It isn't having talent, but deploying the most talented people in the right roles that gives your company strategic advantage and then inspiring them to superior performance. Heckman shares his vast wisdom and experience in enabling organizations to develop their superior talent."

—BILL GEORGE
Harvard Business School Professor,
former Medtronic CEO

"RJ Heckman practices what he preaches. His talent solutions start with the leadership needed to execute strategy, he brings data on people and teams to the conversation, and his thoughts are practical at implementation. If you are trying to align talent with execution to get better results, this is your book."

—DR. MARC BITZER
Chief Executive Officer
Whirlpool Corporation

"Heckman presents a simple and powerful approach for what organizations really need—a coherent and unified perspective to create real value for CEOs and CHROs. An essential 'compass and navigation chart' for all business folks who mean 'business'!"

—SATISH PRADHAN
former Group Head of HR
Tata Group

"A must-read for CEOs and CHROs eager to transform with intention their talent strategy in order to optimize their business performance, while navigating through a hypercompetitive global landscape."

—CHANTAL VEEVAETE
retired SVP of
Human Resources, Phillips 66

THE
TALENT
MANIFESTO

THE
TALENT
MANIFESTO

HOW DISRUPTING PEOPLE
STRATEGIES MAXIMIZES
BUSINESS RESULTS

RJ HECKMAN PhD

New York   Chicago   San Francisco   Athens
London   Madrid   Mexico City   Milan
New Delhi   Singapore   Sydney   Toronto

1 2 3 4 5 6 7 8 9   LCR   24 23 22 21 20 19

ISBN   978-1-260-14254-9
MHID   1-260-14254-X

e-ISBN   978-1-260-14255-6
e-MHID   1-260-14255-8

Library of Congress Cataloging-in-Publication Data
Names: Heckman, RJ, author.
Title: The talent manifesto : how disrupting people strategies maximizes
   business results / by RJ Heckman.
Description: New York : McGraw-Hill, [2019]
Identifiers: LCCN 2018046214 | ISBN 9781260142549 (alk. paper) |
   ISBN 126014254X
Subjects: LCSH: Manpower planning. | Personnel management. | Strategic
   planning.
Classification: LCC HF5549.5.M3 H43 2019 | DDC 658.3/01—dc23
LC record available at https://lccn.loc.gov/2018046214

McGraw-Hill Education books are available at special quantity discounts to use as premiums and sales promotions or for use in corporate training programs. To contact a representative, please visit the Contact Us pages at www.mhprofessional.com.

CONTENTS

PART 1

Principles of the Talent Manifesto

PART 2

Applying the Principles to Talent Processes

PART 3
Bringing It All Together

ACKNOWLEDGMENTS

This project would have never happened without the love and support of my family. My wife, Eileen, and children Ella and Nick are the daily source of my energy and drive to be "BeTTY" (better today than yesterday). My parents and sister, Carrie, are great leaders and talent practitioners who have had success implementing the principles in this book. In many ways I am walking down their well-worn paths as provocateurs and entrepreneurs. I thank my entire family for providing me with the opportunity and support to chase my dreams.

My professional experiences have been many, varied, and rich due to collaborations with dedicated colleagues from all over the world at legacy Personnel Decisions International and Korn Ferry since it acquired PDI. Our organization is filled with brilliant people who help organizations to optimize performance through talent every day. This book started as a collaboration years ago with a good friend and colleague, Dennis Jones. Like me, Dennis drew his ideas as much from his work as a CEO as from his consulting and academic experiences. His ability to integrate great ideas into a meaningful and practical whole that improves individuals' lives and organizational performance is second to none. Although he is now retired, I am grateful that some of his ideas, humor, and creativity will live on in this book.

Other contributors to this book who deserve thanks include my assistant, Katelin Shiels, whose tireless efforts to edit drafts and keep a wide range of client and writing commitments on track have helped me to hit editorial and publisher deadlines. I also thank the McGraw-Hill staff, especially Donya Dickerson and Amy Li, for taking a risk on me as a first-time author. Finally, I appreciate the guidance and written contributions of Dave Zielinski, who partnered with me to complete a variety of projects over the last few years.

Of course, this book would not have been possible without the partnership and support of the client organizations that push me to become better and that have embraced *The Talent Manifesto* as the way to strategically manage their people. We've collected data on more than 20 million professionals from our work with 98 percent of the Fortune 100 and thousands of other organizations around the world. Many of these great companies contributed to this book by sharing the reasons for their talent successes and failures. From them I continue to learn, and for them I am forever grateful.

THE
TALENT
MANIFESTO

INTRODUCTION

Why do some leaders and organizations succeed when others fail?

We've all seen visionary leaders with great ideas. Leaders who are brilliant, charismatic, extremely hard-working, who always operate with integrity. Some of these leaders succeed, but despite enormous talent so many others are unable to build an organization of people that consistently beat the competition.

If you are reading this book, you've also seen human resources (HR) leaders with extraordinary academic credentials and a depth of expertise in HR that took a lifetime to build. Many of these leaders have received awards from HR magazines and associations for the distinguished functional work that they led. Very few, however, understood the financial and strategic opportunities in their organizations so well that they could design and execute talent strategies that produce industry-shattering returns for shareholders. After all, how often is it written that a chief human resources officer's (CHRO) genius for business and talent was the reason for a corporate victory?

It has been said that "the most important conversation about talent strategy has nothing to do with talent," so just find a great business strategy and results will fall into place. Conversely it has also been said that "people create and execute business strategy," so get the right team in place and they will stitch together a great organization. Because both could be argued as correct, I believe the only way to truly drive organizational performance is to sustain a passionate focus on the intersection of business and talent, to require that all decisions about people fall out from that point of intersection, and to never allow focus to run askew.

Yet it happens all the time. Otherwise capable leaders do not accurately distill the talent implications of a strong business strategy. Or in doing so, they inevitably lose focus and allow other things to get in the way. Sometimes even great leaders who truly understand the mission, vision, strategy, and financial reality of their business somehow look away. They look away when they see key positions filled by the wrong people, or they look away when they know there's a big problem with their business but put off implementing a new solution because they have too much on their plate. Often even the best HR leaders make politically expedient decisions, continue ineffective practices because their organization has "always done it this way," or become so enamored with how much others "enjoyed" an initiative they designed that they lack the fortitude to swap the popular with the painful and deliver more impact. Laser focus is often lacking, and the confidence required to be unapologetic when reallocating talent spend to higher-impact investments is very rarely seen. Because of these and many other common leadership challenges, great leaders who fail to focus on the intersection of strategy and talent end up suboptimizing the performance of their organization.

On their best days leaders are confident that their strategies are differentiated and staffed with just the right mix of talent. They can say with certainty that their top teams are going to execute with aplomb. During these times there is a feeling that every action taken and dollar spent is in direct support of accomplishing business objectives. When operating in this sweet spot, data gathered sheds light on decisions that need to be made to drive improvements in performance. In this analytical zone, confidence is built by numbers that predict and explain desired outcomes. When talent and strategy are dancing together, talent processes built to support the business and experiences realized for stakeholders become streamlined, simple, fast, and maybe even fun.

This book demonstrates how to realize that potential and optimize performance so that people and organizations win. The premise is that this can only happen when strategy and talent are in harmony. The recipe for creating this harmony is one-part business strategy, one-part data analytics, and at least one-part simplicity in the user experience for all involved.

Yet despite its simplicity there are many ways to get this recipe wrong. When this happens, time and money are wasted, and performance is unacceptable. At their worst a bad mix of these ingredients will cost people their jobs and may also destroy purpose, performance, and the very existence of an otherwise fine organization.

Background

I don't identify myself as an HR guy.

This was not always the case. I grew up loving the field of HR. My parents were HR practitioners who regularly discussed the reality that people make or break the success of any organization. I couldn't wait to start my first HR generalist role at Graco, Inc., a mid-sized industrial business, where I would learn the technical details of how to hire, evaluate, compensate, develop, and retain people. As valuable a foundation as these lessons were, I quickly learned the exponential value of strong leadership on business performance as I saw a powerful CEO drive increases in human, operational, and financial performance that in turn delivered growth in market capitalization which far exceeded that of his industry competitors and S&P 500 benchmarks overall. I was thrilled when this same CEO, George Aristides, asked me to take an expat assignment in Tokyo to help integrate a recent acquisition and then later pulled me out of HR to work directly for him, "reengineering" parts of the business. The global experience and business perspective I gained under his watch and the tutelage I received from a veteran HR leadership team shaped my views on strategy and talent in ways that will never be forgotten.

I earned a bachelor's degree in psychology from the University of Wisconsin but found myself more interested in the practical application of the classes in the business school. During my tenure at Graco, the company paid for early graduate work at the top-rated HR master's degree program in the United States—the Carlson School of Management at the University of Minnesota. This built the foundation for my technical knowledge of all things HR, but I wanted to see more, do more, and learn as much as I could. I believed that if people create and execute strategy, then I could crack the code on how to select and develop the talent needed for any organization to win.

But from what I had seen, not all organizations win, and in fact, many lose. They go bankrupt, failing to see that competitors are stealing their customers by either out-innovating, out-marketing, out-hustling, out-spending, or under-pricing . . . and in doing so they put otherwise strong organizations out of business. You've probably seen this too, at your own company or in your competitive landscape. This doesn't only happen to smaller organizations—only 60 of the companies on the original Fortune 500 list in 1955 remained on that list in 2017.[1] As these businesses go, their people go too. Either they are laid off because their employer was outwitted, or they get stuck in a dead-end job, underperforming, not realizing their potential, disengaged, overqualified, and often underpaid. Sadly, this is far too common in the world today.

Realizing that this was a problem and not content to roll the dice of chance by signing up with an employer who didn't have what it takes to thrive long-term and then risk losing my own job, but still hungry to learn more about how people impact business performance, I embarked on a journey to better understand one central question: "Why do some people and companies succeed when others fail?"

In search of answers, I left Graco, Inc., and the University of Minnesota and enrolled in a PhD program in industrial/organizational psychology at the University of Tulsa. Among many other classes I took several semesters of statistics and was taught how to use data to prove or disprove the impact of any HR initiative. Concurrent to learning the theoretical I wanted to get to the factual.

While earning my doctorate, I sought to learn what the largest organizations did to improve people and organizational performance. I worked with AT&T on selection systems that would ensure its people had the

top sales talent in the industry. Then I joined a large diversified industrial company, AlliedSignal (which has since bought and taken the name
Honeywell). These large-company experiences provided me an insider
view into how the biggest and best organizations in the world manage
financial and human capital.

My experience has been that with few exceptions the talent practices in mid-sized companies like Graco are very similar to those found
at Honeywell and AT&T. Yet in each organization (and the hundreds of
other leading companies where I have consulted), we find nonstrategic
practices that waste time and money. As a result, people and organizational performance are suboptimized.

My next career stop was joining the consulting ranks of Personnel
Decisions International (PDI). My hope was that clients who were willing
to pay thousands of dollars a day for expertise in managing talent would
indeed be world-class performers. For the most part this is true. Clients
who implemented our recommendations *do* demonstrate stronger performance (this data will be presented in several different chapters where
I show the differences in growth rates, market capitalization, and overall
shareholder return of those companies that practice world-class methods
compared with those that do not). Yet still too few companies do the hard
work required to become best-in-class.

Excited by the innovative clients who were best in class but frustrated
that there were too few such organizations, I set out to lead a company
that would put all its effort, across 30 global operating offices, into helping
organizations perform better. It was then that I became I became president and CEO of PDI.

Only after I landed this top job did I realize just how difficult it was to
optimize people and organizational performance. The reality is that the
role of the CEO is so difficult and the challenges so multifaceted that people issues often get subordinated to portfolio decisions, capital allocations,
sales and distribution opportunities, legal conflicts, and/or operational
fires. As a CEO, I finally realized how quickly the "ideal talent system" was
rendered impractical by economic headwinds, well-funded competitors,

or other common challenges that at any time may threaten the survival of an organization.

I learned the hard way that "disrupting people strategies to maximize business performance" requires a delicate mixture of strategic talent management, data-based insights into people and operations, *and* the common sense to get things done fast and well. *The Talent Manifesto* was written with these considerations in mind. It is a written declaration of what is practical and impactful across organizations and situations, and it was written to shine a bright light on why some leaders and organizations succeed where others fail.

Perhaps You're Not My Target Audience

This book is written for those people primarily responsible for making an organization's most important talent decisions: this may be C-suite executives, their HR partners, or other "talent leaders" at any level or function who are passionate about the role of people in driving a successful enterprise. It is for those who have neither the time nor the inclination to delve into the historical roots of industrial/organizational psychology or business management theory and have no interest, whatsoever, in understanding (for example) how much incremental validity is realized when cognitive abilities testing is added to the use of personality inventories in a selection algorithm. Their only concern is how to improve individual and organizational performance.

This book is written for those who already know that the world of work is changing and that the job of leading others is vastly different today than it was a decade ago. They realize that it will be even more different 10 years from now. It is written for those who already know that the world is *volatile, uncertain, complex, and ambiguous* but want to know how to lead in this VUCA world and still deliver growth in revenue and profitability that beats their competition.

This book will be unsatisfactory for many academically oriented, research-minded colleagues, whom I love dearly, but who seem satisfied to look at the world of work as a glass half empty. Colleagues who seem to see greater danger in oversimplifying the knowledge we have accumulated about talent management than in the danger that comes from always, always talking about how much we don't know. They are right, of course. There is much that we do not know, but in the meantime, leaders still have decisions to make and organizations to run. I strongly hope that professors will give this book a chance by requiring that their students read and discuss its contents, as I believe that it contains important information and case studies that can help them. Today.

This book will be annoying to many senior executives who delegate their organization's talent management problems to HR, and to managers or supervisors who don't spend the time coaching their employees but hold people responsible for poor performance. A central message of this book is that many talent management efforts fail because the senior executives fail. They fail to create a business strategy that defines how the organization is going to drive a strategic competitive advantage. They fail to work with their HR staff and line managers to ensure the correct identification of the talent pools most important for the execution of their business strategy. Incidentally, they also frequently don't know how to coach, and they may be afraid to hold people accountable for changing processes, businesses, or even themselves. They may also lack the skills to communicate a vision that inspires people to perform at levels they never thought possible.

But there is good news. Many times, organizations change from the middle, not the top. It helps when senior executives are enlightened and are willing to face their own developmental challenges directly, but this is not the sole, determining factor. Change can and does happen when the people in the middle make a conscious decision that they have a responsibility to be the best leader they can be, no matter how inadequate or unskilled the people are above them. Change can and does happen when a group of leaders decide there are things that they need to know, skills they need to improve, and values they will honor, regardless of where they work or whom they work for. This book is written for them.

Good Is Not the Enemy of Great

It could be that leaders already know the important things they need to know about talent management. They just don't see it. Wise leaders tell us that the beginning of every transformation begins with the ability to "see." Seeing and knowing are different sides of the coin of understanding, and, in my experience, is the difference between a good and a great manager.

Good managers know that talent is important. Great managers see that the definition of talent changes rapidly and that the people who were "A-players" two years ago are struggling this year. Not because the person has changed (although that does happen), but because the focus of the business has changed, or the economy has changed, or the organization is evolving. New ventures need entrepreneurs. Established businesses need to force cost containment until they need entrepreneurs again. Great leaders see that most of us can only do a few of the dances required for the organization to be successful. They see that only a few of us can do all the dances. Very few.

Good leaders know that people who are smart can move to higher levels of performance quicker than people who are not as smart. Great managers see that being smart must be combined with the ability to get along with others in order to achieve high levels of sustained performance. They also see that people who can get along with others but who cannot make the hard decisions, produce results, or learn quickly are dangerous. Unfortunately, the demand for talented "slow dancers" who "see" but won't act is low these days.

Good leaders know that the ability to make correct decisions about hiring, managing, developing, and promoting is key to their success. Great managers see that correct decisions are not based primarily on intuition but on data, and they demand to see as many facts as possible to inform their decisions. Then they use their "gut" to plot a course of action influenced by data collected.

I disagree with what Jim Collins wrote in his book *Good to Great*. Good is not always the enemy of great. Good is a prerequisite of great. From the perspective of talent management, the challenge is to help otherwise good managers see how to become great leaders.

Human Resource Management Versus Talent Management

The difference between human resource management and talent management is focus. HR leaders must establish personnel systems for all employees in compliance with the laws of the country where the work occurs. There must be guidelines, policies, and procedures in place that establish rules by which people are hired, evaluated, compensated, rewarded, and promoted. These rules must be consistently applied and adhered to, in order to ensure that the organization is not exposed to legal ramifications or public scorn. The HR system is designed to control and minimize differentiation. An organization's human resource management system (HRMS) is widely viewed as synonymous with its talent management system. But the two are not the same. HRMSs are a necessary but not sufficient part of talent management. The measure of an effective HRMS is the alignment of process and practice so that, among other things, compliance is realized and legal exposure is minimized. The measure of an effective talent management system is quality of performance by specific talent pools designated as critical to the success of the organization. HRMSs are primarily focused on processes to manage people. Talent management's focus is one step higher—the management of the talent needed to drive organizational success.

The complexity of talent management decreases significantly when an organization understands the intent of talent management: to focus on escalating the precision of talent decisions often necessary only for a small segment of the employee population and not everyone in the organization. Here the focus must be on driving revenue growth, profitability, and all contributions that create an organization's sustainable competitive advantage. To think in this manner is to strategically and financially optimize the assets in an organization.

Your Most Important Asset

It is really quite simple. People are not your organization's most important asset. *Talented* people are your organization's most important asset. And *untalented* people are a pain in the asset. Untalented people are important, but if you can't (or won't) make decisions that differentiate between the talented and the untalented, you will fail. The problem, of course, is that the definition of talent changes as the business changes. At least it does in organizations that are successful. If your organization is not changing, you can stop reading here. Go back to work. I cannot help you.

Chapter Overview

Part 1 of this book addresses the three principles that serve as the building blocks for *The Talent Manifesto*. The first chapter details the criticality of aligning business and talent strategies. There is little need to discuss talent until the business mission, vision, and strategic differentiators are clearly defined. Before boxes in an organization chart can be filled, tough choices need to be made related to how the business will win in the marketplace. Next, the talent requirements needed in order for the business to execute must be quantified and qualified. The first chapter contains talent strategies that have worked to unleash the potential of many of the finest organizations in the world.

In the second chapter, a major weakness in the field of HR is tackled—talent analytics. Data-based objectivity related to people decisions is sorely lacking. This chapter includes a summary of the prevalence and efficacy of analytics in HR, presents a maturity model for building an analytics strategy, discusses the criticality of data integrity, and ponders the art of the possible when looking across people data sets to deliver game-changing impact on business performance.

The third chapter of the book addresses the critical need to improve the user experience for HR, candidates, employees, and leaders. I share lessons learned from non-HR functions and different companies about what not to do, summarize the perspective of why so many hate HR, and offer alternatives. This chapter also addresses the need for speed. Let's face it—few HR leaders are known to be fleet of foot, and many are the last ones to the change table. A better user experience, executed much faster, is the focus of ideas, research, and recommendations in this chapter.

Part 2 is all about how to apply the principles of Part 1 related to strategy, data, and simpler user experiences when reshaping core talent processes. Chapters in Part 2 include performance management, learning and development, succession planning, compensation, talent acquisition, employee engagement, and the role of HR technology. Keeping up with the pace of change in our ever smaller and more competitive world will not happen until these core talent processes become more strategic, data-driven, and are executed in an integrated way at a much faster pace.

Part 3 of this book brings the principles together with the talent processes and shares perspective on how to make it all happen with excellence. Chapter 11 details the role of boards in providing the leadership and governance needed for success at the intersection of strategy and talent. This chapter also contains insight from directors at some of the largest companies in the world revealing how they've overcome financial, cyber, and environmental crises and social media blunders to maintain high performance at the board and executive levels.

The last chapter presents the "talent waltz," a three-part framework so organizations never miss a beat in applying the principles of strategy, data, and simplicity. Included in this chapter is a case study from another world-class organization, Johnson & Johnson, detailing how it has executed the principles of *The Talent Manifesto* with extraordinary success.

I hope that you enjoy *The Talent Manifesto* and will share your feedback with me as you implement these ideas.

PART 1

PRINCIPLES OF THE TALENT MANIFESTO

CHAPTER 1

TALENT STRATEGY

W hen telecom giant AT&T made the momentous decision to transform itself into a digital business, top executives there understood it would take more than replacing the company's network of telephone switches and fiber-optic cables with a new software-driven infrastructure to make that leap. It would require a wholesale reskilling of the organization's incumbent workforce to drive the new strategy.

The move from landlines to mobile networks created a challenge for executives that went far beyond replacing infrastructure. Research conducted internally found that 100,000 of AT&T's employees worked in roles the company wouldn't need within a decade.[1] Recruiting externally to close identified gaps in software and engineering talent was deemed impractical, given the scale of jobs involved and the relative dearth of outside talent. So AT&T executives launched a billion-dollar employee retraining initiative, the likes of which have rarely been seen in corporate America.

AT&T partnered with a respected university and online education company to create a master's degree program in computer science, giving existing employees access to cutting-edge technology content and top instructors that would help them transition into new roles within the company.[2] AT&T also created a new apprenticeship program and an enterprisewide learning portal and assigned coaches to guide employees as they acquired new digital skills. These initiatives helped AT&T employees transition from roles like retail sales consultant and billing manager to data scientist or scrum master on software development teams.

Amid this transformation, AT&T's leadership team discovered what many other executives in this age of recurring change have yet to realize: talent strategy is just as crucial as financial, marketing, or operational strategies in driving future success. The ability to develop, recruit, and retain the right people—at high velocity—to fill talent gaps created by the evolving business strategy is a DEFCON 1-level priority.

Growing Importance of Talent Strategy

AT&T's experience illustrates how talent management has moved from a tangential, "check-the-box" exercise to an urgent priority for more CEOs as their industries are disrupted by change. When the *Harvard Business Review* recently asked 24 high-profile CEOs to name their biggest challenges, "talent management" topped that list.[3] Those leaders weren't alone when it came to their anxiety over talent matters. Chief executives participating in a Conference Board survey of CEO concerns also placed issues like dealing with labor shortages and creating a culture of engagement high on their priority lists.[4]

Having the right talent, fully engaged, in the right position with the right compensation, so their businesses can stave off competitors, has become a paramount concern for CEOs—an issue as likely to give them cold sweats at night as the prospect of missing their quarterly numbers. Many of the CEOs interviewed for the *HBR* article wanted assurances that they had the right talent in place during periods of organizational change or growth. CEOs who were implementing new digital strategies, for example, said that the swift pace of change had created significant skill gaps in their companies. These leaders understand that their future success likely will be determined by an ability to transform their organizations not just once but continuously, and that rapidly recruiting or developing the right talent to drive those changes will be crucial.

Other executives in the *HBR* survey wondered if they'd have talent that was mobile enough—and equipped with the right cultural intelligence—

to support global expansion. Another segment of surveyed CEOs fretted over whether their high-potential employees were being properly identified and developed for future leadership roles.

Constant, disruptive change represents a new normal for organizations and requires talent strategies that are more agile and data-driven to support shifts in business strategy. Creating the right talent strategy is an intricate and challenging task, especially so when a business strategy becomes a moving target. Job roles and talent needs are changing so quickly in some industries that accurately forecasting future skills needed requires a new level of insight from both human intelligence and predictive analytics software. Such prognostication demands real-time labor market knowledge and the deep learning that the latest artificial intelligence or workforce modeling tools can provide.

There is a symbiotic relationship between talent strategies and business strategies. The fact is, an organization cannot hope to use people management as a competitive lever until it has first crafted a strategy that distinguishes itself in the market. The dirty little secret of talent management is that many talent strategies fail because senior leaders fail at this critical first juncture in the continuum—the creation of highly differentiated and potent business strategies.

The majority of organizations use a strategic planning philosophy with a first step that creates a three-to-five-year strategy, a plan describing how the company will adapt and change to remain at the top of its game.

A second management system typically generates an annual operating plan where quarterly or yearly revenue and budget targets that align with overarching strategy are established.

The third management system that fewer executive teams implement is a people strategy, which examines whether they have the right talent to execute the strategy and hit financial goals. Unfortunately, these analyses rarely include objective and predictive data or direct links of actions back to impact on business strategy. This is an alarming problem given how vital having the right talent in the right place is to executing static or fluid business strategies.

Speed also matters more than ever in today's business operations. Organizations that compete effectively on speed often create talent strategies concurrent with annual operating plans, not as a sequential process or afterthought. Just as the five-year strategic business plan is growing obsolete, so too are talent strategies that aren't agile or responsive enough to meet shifting, near-term skill or knowledge needs that are increasingly tied to business transformations.

Consider the challenge faced by CEOs, CHROs, and talent leaders today. These executives have to move quickly to create the optimal blend of people, artificial intelligence, and machines in the workplace, requiring a fundamental rethinking of how human capital is allocated. Some of the most vexing workplace planning questions of the future won't be about what type of talent to hire, but whether to hire more people at all and whether to offshore, outsource, or implement more automation. When and where in the organization will humans still be more valuable, productive, or cost-efficient than AI, robotics, or other automated tools?

A Five-Step Approach to Creating Talent Strategies

Companies that implement the following five-step approach to creating talent strategy are more likely to build effective plans and execute their business strategies with distinction:

1. Crystallize the talent implications of your business strategy.
2. Create the right organizational structure and culture for talent strategies to thrive.
3. Identify the organization's pivotal roles with precision.
4. Specifically define success profiles for pivotal roles.
5. Make data-driven "buy-versus-build" decisions to close key talent gaps.

Create Alignment with Business Strategy

The origin of any effective talent strategy lies in an agreement between the CEO and CHRO on a differentiated business strategy. Will it be based on digitization? Operational excellence? Customer intimacy? Innovation? Organic growth or growth through acquisition? Clarifying the strategy lays the groundwork for the critical decisions that CHROs and executive teams must make around closing talent gaps and strengthening organizational capabilities to support the strategic direction.

Taking a research-based approach to identifying the specific talent needs and organizational capabilities required to execute business strategy creates talent investments with the greatest payoff. If digitization is the strategy, for example, does the company have the right organizational design, talent, and incentives in place to foster that approach? Are there creative and rigorous recruiting processes to attract talent with digital skills? Do the right development, compensation, and retention strategies exist to keep that valuable talent on board once in place?

Figure 1.1 shows how business strategies should drive the talent and organizational capabilities needed to create and sustain a competitive advantage.

Consider how organizations like AT&T, Best Buy, Nordstrom, and Apple designed talent strategies to support their differentiated—and in some cases evolving—business strategies. As detailed in this chapter's opening, AT&T underwent a digital transformation as its customers disconnected landlines en masse and shifted to mobile devices, forcing the telecom company to replace legacy hardware with new software systems. That overhaul required that the workforce acquire an array of new technical skills to succeed, and AT&T's executives responded with a bold new initiative to retrain existing staff for new roles in the redesigned company.

When electronics retailer Best Buy responded to new pressure from its competitors by repositioning its business strategy, HR leaders in the company had to quickly adjust talent strategy to support the change. The revamped operating strategy stressed improved in-store customer service

FIGURE 1.1   The KF business-talent strategy decoder

CRITICAL TALENT ORGANIZATIONAL CAPABILITIES

Foundational   **ORGANIZATIONAL PRIORITY / IMPACT**   Strategic

BUSINESS STRATEGIES		
Board Governance	Succession Management	Diversity and Inclusion
Top Team Effectiveness	Success Profiles/Competencies	Collaboration
Employer Branding	Total Rewards	Execution
Workforce Planning	Integrated Talent Processes	Organizational Design
Talent Acquisition and Recruitment	HR Function	Organizational Agility and Transformation
Talent Engagement	Cultural Values, Behaviors, Practices	Functional Excellence
Talent Development and Deployment	Open Communication	Customer Intimacy
Performance Management	Knowledge Management	Brand Embodiment

■ Higher Organizational Skill/Effectiveness   ▨ Moderate Organizational Skill/Effectiveness   ▨ Lower Organizational Skill/Effectiveness

and highlighted the services of the Geek Squad, an elite team of information technology experts.[5] In response, HR put retail employees through a retraining boot camp and focused recruiting and retention efforts on fortifying the Geek Squad. Those initiatives rebooted the company and generated strong new revenues through sales of connected-home solutions that leveraged the recent developments of products enabled by the "Internet of Things."

These efforts have clearly paid dividends. At a time when other electronics and appliance companies are going bankrupt in droves, Best Buy is thriving and its market capitalization is currently soaring at an all-time high. Another example of Best Buy's market savvy was when its CEO Hubert Joly recently appeared together with his chief rival, Jeff Bezos (CEO of Amazon), to announce their joint respect for one another's business and agreed to partner in the sales and marketing of a new connected TV.

In providing unparalleled customer service via the Geek Squad and redefining the in-store experience provided by store associates, Best Buy integrated its people and business strategies. As a result, it is performing well and (at least for the time being) staving off the fierce online competitors.

Here are a few more examples: To drive a strategy based on customer intimacy, retailer Nordstrom tailored its recruiting, development, and compensation systems for the purpose of hiring, incentivizing, and retaining talent with elite customer service skills. Apple famously tethered its talent strategy to a business model dependent on hiring the world's top innovators to create breakthrough products—and then went to great lengths to keep those individuals producing at high levels for Apple, not a rival.

Making talent strategy a focal point rather than an afterthought in driving business strategy is essential in today's disruptive business environment. Repositioning your company with this in mind ensures that the vital link between talent and business outcomes is given proper attention in an executive team's off-site planning meetings, granting talent issues equal standing to strategic, operational, or budgeting issues.

As business strategies evolve, CHROs also need to recalibrate talent strategies to keep pace with the changes. If a company's strategy shifts to emphasize digitization, for example, HR leaders must ensure they have the right quality and quantity of talent in place to support the change. Rapidly hiring those tech-savvy workers—or retraining existing staff for a skills pivot—can mean the difference between a business strategy thriving or failing.

Identify the Role of Organizational Structure

CHROs and talent leaders also need to work with the executive team to assess the organizational moorings that allow business and talent strategies to thrive. That includes devising the best structure for the organization to operate within and building a culture that supports the execution of a differentiated business strategy.

Recent studies suggest companies are more focused than ever on redesigning their organizations to support business strategies. For example, organizational design was deemed the most important trend in consulting firm Deloitte's two latest Global Human Capital Trends surveys. As organizations become more digital, they face a growing need to redesign themselves to move faster, adapt more quickly, facilitate rapid learning, and embrace the new career demands of their workforces, the surveys found.[6]

Only 14 percent of executives in the studies believed that the traditional, industrial-age organizational design model, based on hierarchical job levels tied to expertise in given areas, makes their organizations more effective and competitive. Many were considering adopting more adaptable, team-centric models with units that could be formed and disbanded quickly around specific projects.

Poorly conceived organizational design can neutralize expensive efforts to hire or develop top talent. For example, a hierarchy-oriented structure characterized by management control and stability won't support a talent strategy designed to hire large numbers of millennials or generation Z workers who thrive on fast-moving environments, collaboration, and open communication with executives. Similarly, if the goal of a business strategy is to bring new products to the market faster, but the organization is designed in functional silos that inhibit cross-functional collaboration, organizational structure will put a brake on strategy execution.

Organizations may sometimes use this straightforward three-step process as part of their restructuring efforts:

1. List the top strategic challenges facing your business in columns on a spreadsheet.
2. List the people considered your top leaders in the rows of the same spreadsheet.
3. Match one row with one column based on expertise and personal passion.

This approach can be elegant in its simplicity, but it is not sufficient when addressing the broader cross-functional challenges of growth, innovation, or operational excellence in today's global organizations; still it is appealing when trying to KISS (keep it simple stupid).

Organizational structure is not a one-and-done. Design often needs to change to support evolving business and talent strategies. For example, if a CHRO forecasts a need for more leaders with profit-and-loss management experience but sees inadequate bench strength in that area, he or she might suggest reorganizing divisions to create new roles with smaller P&L, cross-functional, or project management responsibilities. That experience will help prepare leaders for broader bottom-line accountability in the future.

To transition faster into digitization, a CEO and CHRO might need to work together to reconstitute "success profiles" for certain job roles, create new work teams, or form special units with expertise in that area. Likewise, a shift to a more consultative selling strategy could require the creation of a dedicated sales team to serve key accounts.

Consider how technology leader Adobe changed its organizational structure to help develop and engage talent. Adobe's top HR leader, Donna Morris, was put in charge of both handling the employee and customer experience and overseeing Adobe facilities. Shifting the company structure this way allows Morris to manage two of the company's most valuable but high-cost assets—organizational talent and buildings—in a way that better served Adobe's strategy and customers. As a result, Morris was able to reassign key talent to growing global markets, consolidate facilities, and create new advancement opportunities for employees like software engineers. These moves energized and engaged employees, boosting customer service and financial results in the process.

Sync Talent Strategy with Culture

Changes in business strategy also require executive teams to revisit organizational culture and ensure that it remains aligned with operational goals. The need to reconsider culture is illustrated in the acquisition of Hillshire Brands by Tyson Foods. Integrating the brands, processes, and culture of

Hillshire Brands with that of Tyson created the kind of new growth avenues and higher margins for the combined company that would have been difficult to achieve had they remained separate. One driving force behind the merger's success was Tyson's CHRO, Mary Oleksiuk, who together with her HR team worked to unify the new business strategy with the culture and mission of the combined company.

Oleksiuk's human resources group helped to engage and unite five generations of employees behind the joint company's mission of "making great food, making a difference." That unification and evolved culture contributed to a doubling of the organization's market capitalization within two years of the merger.

Identify Pivotal Roles

More than 10 years ago, Boudreau and Ramstad introduced a new concept to the HR community.[7] The strategic logic in their thinking is undeniably deep, but HR leaders' execution and integration of their concepts has been spotty. Pivotal job roles are those in which enhancing the quality and/or quantity of talent has a disproportionate impact on business success. The term conjures thoughts of top executives, sales leaders, marketing heads, or other key managers. While those jobs are clearly important, pivotal talent can come in many sizes and shapes. Depending on the industry, organization, and business strategy, critical roles might also include software developers, artificial intelligence specialists, street sweepers, gate crews for airlines, real estate analysts, front-desk service staff, or maintenance mechanics. Pivotal roles also can be geography-dependent. If a growth strategy involves expanding into Mexico, China, or India, for example, certain commercial or leadership roles in those countries might be deemed more pivotal than the same role in other countries.

HR leaders are often surprised when they find—following a workforce analysis that determines which job roles have the biggest impact on key operating metrics—which positions qualify as pivotal and which do not.

Favoring some job roles over others also runs counter to the time-honored belief in human resources about the equitable treatment of all employees. *But courageous CHROs don't shy away from the reality that some roles are far more important than others in driving competitive advantage.* Rather than trying to spread limited recruiting, development, or compensation resources equally across all employees, these CHROs allocate resources in ways that favor the attraction, development, and retention of incumbents in pivotal positions.

One example of allocating resources in this fashion comes from pharmacy company CVS Health. CHRO Lisa Bisaccia and her team designated the pharmacist position as a pivotal role in the organization. Pharmacists were deemed both "quality" pivotal—given that prescription sales represent more than half of company revenues and even small mistakes on the pharmacists' part can harm valued customers and the company brand—and "quantity" pivotal, as the chain employs more than 30,000 pharmacists in its national network.

When I asked Bisaccia how CVS manages so many pivotal pharmacists, she reported that her team has implemented targeted recruiting, engagement, and retention strategies with the goal of ensuring that only the market's top pharmacists were hired and developed into long-tenured employees. Bisaccia manages these pivotal roles using a complex algorithm of staffing, scheduling, and development procedures to ensure the right pharmacists are in the right stores at the right time to enhance customer service and maximize results.

Define Success Profiles with Precision

With talent pools segmented based on the business impact they deliver, CHROs should work with business-line leaders to decide exactly what results are expected and which specific competencies, experiences, traits, and drivers are required for success in pivotal roles. Any one or two of these dimensions are typically not sufficient in precisely defining the right stuff required for these jobs. Taking a "whole-person" approach when recruiting or developing individuals for these positions creates the basis for improved talent management decisions.

Business success can largely be measured by an organization's capacity and courage to make critical decisions that differentiate from competitors not only on business strategy, but also via the defined requirements of success for various talent pools in the organization. Yet too often business-line leaders struggle to translate their talent needs into specific capabilities that help guide HR functions in making recruiting, development, or engagement decisions.

That process improves when line leaders can separate the mission-critical from the "nice-to-have" results and expectations required of each position. This allows HR to convert those desired behaviors and outcomes into job-specific success profiles. For example, the success profile for an information technology executive might assign higher priority to competencies like the use of best-practice data security protocols or experiences like defending IT infrastructure investments to a board. Similarly, a well-constructed success profile for a CHRO might place greater weight on the skills required to deal effectively with the board's compensation, nominating, and governance committees.

A talent framework like Korn Ferry's Four Dimensions of Leadership and Talent (KF4D) helps develop success profiles for pivotal roles based on research identifying what differentiates top performers from other employees (see Figure 1.2). A comprehensive "language of talent" such as this is essential for organizations that are serious about getting aligned on what "exemplary" performance looks like position by position in their companies.

It's also important that HR leaders align with specificity the success profile and the employee value proposition (EVP) for pivotal roles. Given how important it is for incumbents in pivotal roles to succeed, it's critical that the EVP be well aligned, or the business simply won't attract and retain market-leading talent. If a role is pivotal to success, then the EVP must trump what competitors might offer.

FIGURE 1.2   Korn Ferry's Four Demensions of Leadership and Talent

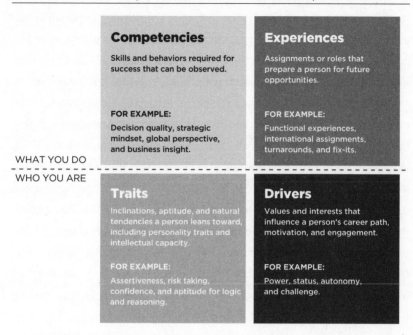

A good EVP incorporates pay and benefits and provides learning and growth opportunities as well as assures work-life balance, an attraction of particular interest to millennials. A next-level EVP also emphasizes how employees will experience a sense of purpose in their work and that their organization's brand and culture will be sources of pride.

Make the Buy-Versus-Build Decision

Using data-driven approaches to identify gaps in pivotal talent pools creates choice points for CHROs and other talent leaders. Will they fill gaps between the talent on hand and the talent required by recruiting externally or by developing existing employees? This high-stakes buy-versus-build decision rests on a number of variables. HR and talent leaders should consider recruiting outside the organization when skills are difficult to develop internally, when there is urgency to fill skill gaps, or when there is no history of needed competencies within a company or department.

For example, HR may have a pressing need for advanced data analytics skills in its own function but no history of employing people with such capabilities. Rather than trying to develop analytics competencies in HR generalists, it may be more expedient to recruit externally or to transfer internal finance or marketing staff with those skills into human resources.

Conversely, developing new skills in incumbent employees to fill talent gaps—the "build" option—may be a better choice when infusing outside talent is deemed risky to the culture, when there are known talent shortages in external candidate pools, or when it can be challenging to recruit to certain geographies or industries. When AT&T reinvented itself to compete in an industry being disrupted by new software-centric business models, HR leaders determined that many of the technical skills needed to support the new strategy weren't available outside the organization. So AT&T opted instead to rapidly reskill its existing workforce by using external partnerships and cutting-edge training techniques and by instituting a culture of perpetual learning.[8]

Many other organizations refuse to promote internal job candidates if they aren't able to outperform external candidates on job-critical skill assessments. HR leaders in these companies seek assurances that their promotion decisions won't result in placing just their own top talent in elevated roles, but rather candidates that ranked best in the overall market.

CEO and CHROs: The Critical Collaboration

When creating talent strategies, it's crucial that CEOs and CHROs collaborate to determine the talent and organizational capabilities essential in supporting a differentiated business strategy. These two leaders should identify how important specific talent pools, organizational structure, culture, and incentive systems are to that strategy. The CHRO's team should then rigorously assess how the company stands in each area. Once that process is complete, HR leaders need to display the courage and influence skills to reallocate talent resources to areas that do most to drive competitive advantage.

Just as CEOs regularly make tough capital reallocation decisions, CHROs should review the data on recruiting, development, promotion, and reward programs and employ a zero-based budgeting approach to fund future talent strategies. Only then will HR executives ensure that their talent strategies are calibrated and aligned in ways that provide the necessary fuel to drive business success.

PERILOUS PITFALLS
Six Obstacles to Creating Effective Talent Strategies

As with any effort to overcome entrenched thinking or time-honored practices, there will be obstacles that stand in the way of HR leaders creating the kind of next-generation talent strategies needed to thrive in today's turbulent markets. Here are some of the biggest pitfalls to which CHROs and talent leaders can fall prey, based on Korn Ferry's research and talent consulting work.

Lack of courage to abandon business-as-usual. Implementing a more proactive and agile talent strategy often requires challenging the status quo and making tough decisions. CHROs need moxie as well as effective negotiating skills—to master the *art of conviction*—to allocate recruiting, development, or compensation resources in new ways or to shelve established HR initiatives that don't support an evolving business strategy.

Decisions like discontinuing long-running training programs that no longer have strategic value, for example, can ruffle feathers. While courting controversy, these are the kind of resource reallocation decisions that CEOs make on a regular basis to keep their organizations healthy. CHROs shouldn't receive a pass on similar decision making.

As Netflix's former chief talent officer Patty McCord has pointed out in her speeches and articles, HR leaders also should

(continued on next page)

strive to be *problem solvers, not problem finders.* Leaders who can point to problems are a dime a dozen, McCord says, but those who can come up with creative and practical solutions represent an organization's true pivotal talent.

Absence of capabilities within HR to deliver on talent strategy. The HR function must be staffed with the right quality and quantity of professionals in the right locations to execute on talent strategies. For example, an HR group that has historically used external recruiting to close certain skill gaps but is shifting to reskilling existing employees for that purpose will need to rethink how it is staffed to best support the change.

Similarly, a new corporate objective to combine workforce and business analytics to improve decision making may require more HR staff with analytics competencies. In another scenario, an organization expanding into new global markets might need HR leaders with international experience to relocate overseas.

One recent study found that high-performing HR teams have fewer generalists and more senior HR partners. HR functions are reskilling existing staff to serve in the latter role, in many cases educating them in the use of digital management practices and digital apps and tools like artificial intelligence to improve recruiting, employee learning, and service delivery.[9] "Being digital" has become a core competency of high-impact HR functions, as many of them also push industry vendors to deliver more user-friendly, mobile-ready, and analytics-rich technology solutions.

Inadequate attention to external influences. Developing talent strategies in isolation of outside influences or intelligence about competitors is dangerously insular. CHROs should monitor the competition to note significant changes in hiring strategies, modifications to incentive programs, or any organizational restructuring. Such changes usually foretell a shift in business strategy.

Talent leaders also need to be well informed on matters like the availability of pivotal talent in locations where business growth opportunities lie, emergent recruiting strategies or technologies that can help identify hard-to-find talent, and regulatory or compliance issues that affect talent strategies.

Unoriginal talent strategies. It can be easy to fall into the trap of creating talent strategies that mimic competitors' approaches or those of best-practice organizations. But talent strategies only succeed when custom-built to serve unique business strategies and organizational cultures. A new strategy focused on external recruiting as a way to fill leadership talent gaps, for example, might be anathema to a culture that's long thrived on home-grown development or promotion of talent. Put your own unique stamp on a talent strategy.

No horizontal alignment of talent processes. Talent strategies can suffer when individual talent processes aren't aligned with one another in support of business strategies. For example, if a recruiting initiative is designed to hire more employees with business development skills but a performance management system doesn't accurately measure the use of those skills—or if reward systems don't adequately incent people for generating new business—performance won't be optimized.

Failure to consider the impact of culture. We've all heard that "culture eats strategy for breakfast," a quote attributed to the late management guru Peter Drucker. Failing to align talent strategies with organizational culture can undermine execution of business strategy. For example, a company with an entre-

(continued on next page)

preneurial culture that is competing on agility and innovation requires a different talent strategy than one with a more bureaucratic culture competing on operational excellence. Effectively leveraging culture is an essential but oft-overlooked component of talent strategy creation.

Review and Action Items

1. There are just as many different talent strategies as there are business strategies. Whether competing on price, innovation, or customer intimacy, it is critical that HR processes deliver the talent needed to execute. Yet too many talent strategies are nondescript or are mere imitations of companies with entirely different challenges. A short, direct line must be made between the allocation of talent resources and execution of business strategy.

2. Talent strategies are multifaceted and must address unique performance drivers related to culture, structure, and the differential impact that pivotal roles have in creating organizational value.

3. Defining talent needs with a level of granularity that clearly specifies the quantity and quality of talent needed will reduce execution risk. When the levels of talent required to support strategy are divorced from the realities of the current capabilities, the creative gap-closing build-versus-buy-versus-partner options—as well as organizational restructuring and even adjusting of business strategies themselves—must be considered.

CHAPTER 2

DATA

Building a "Data-Smart" HR Culture: The Case for Next-Level Talent Analytics

The practice of talent analytics is undergoing a profound shift. With the arrival of new cloud-based analytics technologies and the growing use of modern assessment methods, CHROs and CEOs have more resources than ever at their fingertips. Together, these tools provide more meaningful data about recruiting, performance measurement, compensation, and employee retention.

This new data revolution is rewriting the script for how HR functions can impact organizations, and yet, the reality is that too many HR leaders still remain on the outside looking in. While CHROs have long used analytics to gauge efficiency measures like time to hire, performance evaluations completed, or compliance with government regulations, it remains rare to find the use of advanced analytics that gauge the effectiveness or impact of HR initiatives on organizational performance.

One recent study found that although 83 percent of HR leaders agree that all people decisions should be based on data, only 37 percent use analytics to help solve talent management problems.[1] Another study found that more than half of talent leaders still use manual processes to gather, report, and analyze their data.[2] A third survey found that after years of discussing the need for improved analytics, only 8 percent of companies report they have usable people data, and only 9 percent believe they have a good understanding of which talent dimensions drive performance in their organizations. Just 15 percent have broadly deployed HR and talent scorecards for line managers.[3]

Compare that troubling review with the advanced state of analytics use in functions outside HR and in the consumer world:

- Chief financial officers regularly access real-time financial data and monitor key performance indicators using fully integrated, easy-to-view dashboards. CFOs employ this business intelligence software to analyze financial performance and forecast expenditures across departments and data types without having to juggle multiple spreadsheets.
- Chief marketing officers use advanced analytics to track the performance of lead-generation efforts, branding campaigns, customer purchases, and media buys. These marketing leaders receive a complete picture of audience behaviors and attributes across channels with a few clicks on a single, consolidated analytics platform.
- The analytics revolution has swept through the consumer world as well. It's now easier than ever to use smartphone apps to conduct product or price comparisons, to find the quickest route home on a commute, or to access user reviews of businesses or potential employers. Enormous amounts of data exist online, and companies like Amazon and Netflix provide shortcuts to what's most relevant to consumers' most idiosyncratic tastes at the swipe of a finger.

HR's full participation in this analytics revolution can't come soon enough. CHROs or talent acquisition leaders who use both *quality-of-hire* metrics and analytics that can reliably identify employees who might be overpaid or underpaid in the organization remain in the minority. Similarly, HR functions that track mission-critical measures like the total cost of workforce (TCOW) or that use analytics to predict which groups of employees might collaborate or innovate most effectively together are still the exception.

Forward-thinking CHROs increasingly are beginning to connect the data dots in creative ways (see the sidebar "The Art of the Possible: Realizing the Potential of Talent Analytics" later in this chapter for more on this topic). In today's volatile business climate, where strategies pivot and job roles change with quickening speed, CEOs look with more urgency to CHROs for accurate forecasts of future talent needs, to help devise the right mix of people, artificial intelligence, and automation in the workplace, and to find ways to keep top talent on board and productive. CHROs who can glean insights from mature HR analytics or predictive models to help CEOs and CFOs make these decisions elevate themselves above the pack.

CEOs have good reason for seeking to expand data-driven decision making in their organizations—including within the HR function. One recent study found that *quantified* organizations (those that are data-driven in their decision making) have a 79 percent higher return on equity than nonquantified organizations. Of the 350 companies participating in the study, only 29 were identified as quantified organizations.

The study also found that quantified organizations give leaders and managers direct access to analytics, rather than funneling that access through analytics specialists. The research findings were obtained using aggregated data from publicly traded survey respondents that provided financial data.[4]

Progressive HR functions are moving away from creating dedicated groups of analytics specialists and are instead moving toward embedding analytics capabilities throughout their entire workforce management operations. Their goal: to leverage people data for a broader range of business challenges and decisions, not just for HR problems.

The Missing Link: Data Integrity

Building a "data-smart" culture requires that CHROs closely monitor the integrity of data used to make talent decisions. The reality is that many organizations still struggle with fundamental data collection issues, such as identifying their overall head count, or with the accurate collection of other basic employee records. In addition, the GIGO (garbage in, garbage out) principle remains alive and well in the talent management disciplines.

Numerous research studies show that most leaders are unreliable raters of their subordinates' performances, with a litany of performance rating errors (idiosyncratic rater effect, just like me, central tendency, primacy/recency) contributing to a high rate of flawed talent decisions.

A study of 6,000 managers who were evaluated by two different bosses illustrates the danger of relying too heavily on an individual leader's appraisal.[5] These bosses were asked to rate the managers' competence on a seven-point scale, and of the 15 percent of managers who were rated "outstanding" by one boss, the second boss disagreed 62 percent of the time. That second boss rated the same person "somewhat above average" or lower 29 percent of the time. Of the 17 percent of managers who were rated "average" or lower by one boss, the second boss disagreed 39 percent of the time.

As if this weren't bad enough, a whopping 80 percent of all employees in the survey were rated to be "above average"! This obvious mathematical impossibility should be all the evidence HR leaders need to scrap age-old, inaccurate processes; yet such methods persist in many organizations today.

Too many of the high-stakes decisions made in organizations about whom to hire, develop, promote, or retain are still based on unreliable data and incomplete talent insights. For example, while most managers, like most of the general population, believe they are above-average raters of talent, the research consistently shows otherwise.

With compensation and benefits representing 30 to 70 percent of operating costs in most organizations, vigilant CEOs should have assurances that talent is being hired, assessed, and retained in ways that maximize that considerable investment.[6] Inaccurate performance reviews of talent contribute greatly to driving up compensation costs in companies.

Progressive CHROs understand that the accurate segmentation of talent is essential to best-practice talent management and that inaccurate talent decisions can impact business performance for years. That's why they embrace the use of more rigorous assessment methods—and seek a better balance between science and art in talent evaluation—to increase their odds of making the right choices. In the process they allocate precious company resources just as judiciously as their counterparts in finance, marketing, or the supply chain.

Modern assessment science makes it possible to improve the accuracy of decisions made throughout the talent management life cycle, employing hyperrealistic job simulations, psychometric tests, competitions, and other tools to supplement interviews or reference checks and replace intuition with valid science. High-performing HR organizations prioritize those job roles for which these simulations or multidimensional assessment approaches are critical and allocate resources accordingly.

Data integrity too often is the odd man out in the rush to employ more talent analytics. For example, pre-hire assessment tools designed to evaluate the skills, knowledge, or cultural fit of job candidates may be easy and quick for applicants to complete on smartphones, but when those same assessments lack reliability, validity, or legal defensibility, any gains from their user-friendliness are lost. *In too many cases candidates being evaluated (and then hired) by such assessments exit an organization's back door as quickly as they came through the front door.*

Adding more valid science to decisions around key talent has lasting payoffs for organizations. Executive assessments can reveal, for example, that while someone under consideration for a CEO job might be a great fit for his or her current role managing a single geography or stable business unit, the person might not possess the learning agility or flexibility to make the leap to enterprise leadership in an organization undergoing transformation. (More on this point in Chapter 11 on the role of boards in CEO succession.)

As an example, for the past several years Johnson & Johnson has had Korn Ferry assess internal and external candidates for senior leader roles. Data from the effort has led not only to higher-quality hires but also to insight on how to better support the flourishing of innovation in its businesses. After more than 1,000 such assessments, including interviews, psychometrics, and business simulations, J&J confidently selects leaders across the globe. The assessments deliver data-based comparisons to benchmarks of top leaders from companies known to be the best in the world at innovation. Now J&J HR leaders like Sarah Brock, global leader of assessment and development, have gone from a position of "we think" we are a strategic support to the businesses to "we know" we are delivering actionable data that improves performance for our most pivotal talent that drives innovation.

Consider as well the data collected in a typical performance management process. Data gathered using inconsistent or unreliable processes—and without the benefit of job success profiles that separate mission-critical competencies and experiences from the "nice-to-have" variety—can leave CHROs exposed to challenge. Those challenges come from employees or managers questioning the accuracy of the data or legal disputes about the consistency or relevance of methods used to collect the data.

Forward-thinking organizations continue to move away from the annual performance appraisals toward more frequent, informal "check-ins" to gauge employee performance. This trend toward providing real-time, individualized feedback is largely positive, generating data and impressions about employee performance much sooner after the fact and helping leaders focus as much on improving future performance as on evaluating past results. *But a more modern, user-friendly process holds no guarantees of improved data quality. One recent study found that 90 percent of heads of HR believe their performance management system does not yield accurate information.*[7] That's a significant problem given that the impact of flawed performance management evaluations on compensation decisions, could cost even small companies millions.

For example, many performance management systems still evaluate behaviors or competencies based on a numeric scale, without rating observed behavior in a way that calibrates measurement across multiple raters. The latter process helps compensate for the fact that individual managers are not reliable raters of others' performance. CHROs need to strike the right balance between the user-friendliness of performance reviews and the reliability and validity of data used to make these high-stakes appraisal decisions.

A Talent Analytics Maturity Model: Evolving from Efficiency to Bottom-Line Impact

Talent analytics exist on a maturity continuum with three levels. While analytics at each level play a vital role in measuring HR's impact on an organization, the use of more mature analytics separates strategic HR functions from their more transactionally focused counterparts.

Talent analytics used in most organizations still primarily look backward instead of forward, using metrics to gauge compliance risks or to benchmark against industry or competitor norms. While reviewing past performance yields valuable insights, data-driven HR organizations are twice as likely as their counterparts to look ahead than behind when it comes to talent analytics.[8] These groups use data to help predict outcomes, instead of merely reacting to them.

Here are the three levels of a modified analytics maturity model that was originally proposed by Boudreau and Ramstad.[9] Gauge yourself against each and consider where your organization stands in its own talent analytics journey.

Efficiency Analytics

The majority of analytics used within HR measure *efficiency* and fall into the first stage of the maturity model. These analytics are typically tied to cost, cycle time, compliance, or other transactional measures. Examples include recruiting metrics like time to fill or cost to fill open jobs, service delivery measures like HR response time to employee requests, employee satisfaction with benefits plans, the number of completed training courses, and measures that gauge how the automation of HR processes saves time or reduces labor costs.

Included at this level also are analytics that measure compliance with government rules or regulations that are designed to help CHROs manage risk. Most efficiency metrics are based on *descriptive* statistics—averages, frequencies, and percentages. Descriptives are a necessary part of a strong analytics platform but alone aren't sufficient because they usually don't correlate with or predict any high-value performance factors. For example, knowing that 20 percent more people completed a development plan as part of a career development or succession planning initiative is helpful, but it doesn't mean that learning goals will be realized or that workers will be more effective or engaged on the job. Similarly, reducing turnover by 50 percent seems impressive; but if additional analyses revealed that the departures were, regrettably, a companies' top contributors then the initially positive analyses of reduced turnover would be viewed quite differently!

Effectiveness Analytics

The second level of maturity features analytics that measure *effectiveness,* or how talent decisions and HR resource allocations affect employee or unit performance. The quality of effectiveness analytics is highly dependent on the validity and reliability of the methods used in the measurement process.

One example of an effectiveness measure is quality of hire. Strategic CHROs understand that it does little good to hire employees quickly or inexpensively if they don't perform at consistently high levels over time or if they turn over sooner than desired. These CHROs strive to help line leaders make hiring decisions fast without trading off the appropriate level of assessment rigor.

Some HR leaders shy away from using effectiveness analytics because of the perceived complexity of the measurement process. Yet the reality is that many effectiveness metrics can be implemented with little additional time or investment. The payoff is data and insights that greatly improve future talent management decisions.

Consider what's needed to measure quality of hire. An accurate gauge requires an aggregated index of post-hire metrics such as turnover rates within specified periods or a review of performance appraisals. More advanced approaches might factor in the influence of managers and coworkers beyond the hiring stage. For example, recruiters might be hiring strong candidates, but if managers fail to lead or engage them effectively, it can result in higher-than-average attrition rates.

Such an effectiveness measure also might include analyzing recruiting data to unearth root problems in hiring processes that result in suboptimal hires. Dissecting such data might find, for example, that small teams of recruiters using structured interviews are far more accurate in hiring high performers than large teams with unstructured methods. Further, even the small, structured team could save time and money while increasing candidate quality and user experience by using fewer interviews and inserting the use of engaging psychometrics. In another scenario, comparing the assessment data of newly hired salespeople, for example, against their job performance might show that those scoring at higher levels on assessments in dimensions like the ability to form strong relationships with others, big-picture thinking, and persistence in the face of challenges proved to be better performers than hires who tested lower on assessments for those attributes. Effective hiring processes for other roles, accountants, for example, would be significantly different from the assessment used for salespeople. Understanding both the hiring methods and statistically derived success profiles for those roles is critical.

Effectiveness measures go a step beyond efficiency metrics when meaningful data points statistically correlate significantly with other key measures. Consider for example the relationship between job performance and measures of capabilities including problem solving, personality traits, and/or competencies observed and measured by standardized behavior using assessment tools.

As shown in Figure 2.1, there is value in establishing a mathematical relationship between certain personal attributes identified through assessments and strong post-hire job performances across a large number of people in similar roles. The "readiness assessment" scores of strongly recommended candidates in the graphic correlate positively with the job performance of those candidates 12 to 24 months later.

FIGURE 2-1 Performance ratings

"Strongly recommended" candidates (in light gray) are eight times more likely to be among the top quartile of performers as rated by their supervisors 12 to 24 months later. If the assessments did not predict performance, the graph would be flat, showing an even 25% of leaders in each quartile of performance (illustrated in dark gray).

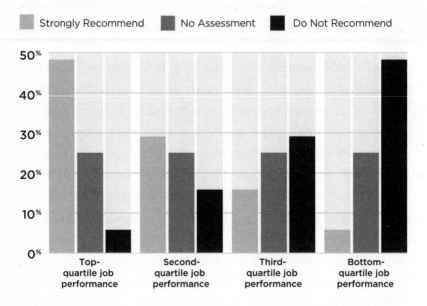

Establishing these relationships is far superior to using descriptive statistics; yet only the strongest HR leaders get this far in their analytics journey.

Here are some examples of effectiveness measures that data-driven HR organizations use, as well as questions often posed in each category:

- Correlation of assessments with future job performance. Do the results of assessments used in making hiring, readiness, promotion, or succession planning decisions correlate accurately with success on the job? How likely are candidates who are strongly recommended for roles based on assessment scores to be in the top tier of performers rather than the middle or bottom tier? (See Figure 2.1.)

- Performance management. How confident are talent leaders that a performance management system accurately differentiates A-, B-, and C-level players in their organization? CHROs are often skeptical about whether their performance data is strong enough to tie it to high-stakes compensation or reward decisions.

- Performance data that is scored to yield summary information can be leveraged to accurately differentiate performance from various perspectives. Examples are percentile rankings within and across groups or stacked rankings of individuals within a pivotal talent pool. Organizations also tend to settle too easily for locally collected information about individual performance to make reward-related decisions. The real power of people data lies in its comparability for driving a talent strategy across the enterprise.

- Measurement of flight risks of pivotal talent. Do flight risk assessments combine workforce data with non-HR data to measure the risk of losing high-performing employees with high potential in pivotal roles (for example, stock option activity combined with recent updating of a LinkedIn profile)?

- Learning and development. Does the organization attempt to measure the impact of formal learning on job or organizational performance, instead of just tracking the completion of classroom or e-learning courses or only compiling posttraining "smile sheets" or test scores?

Impact Analytics

The third and most evolved level of analytics consists of *impact* measures, or HR metrics, that assess and predict outcomes that are central to organizational performance. When well-measured employee performance or potential data is correlated with employee engagement, customer satisfaction, revenue, or profitability, HR functions have reached the pinnacle of analytics.

At this maturity level, for example, performance management data might be integrated with other key business measures (such as financial data) to achieve deeper insight into the relationship between individual or group performance and business outcomes. Here HR also might work with finance to measure the total cost of the workforce to gauge how labor expenses contribute to organizational results.

TCOW metrics typically include salary and benefit costs in addition to labor costs such as recruiting, onboarding, and training. Given that these costs are the largest expense in most companies, it's vital that HR take steps to show how such workforce investments impact bottom-line performance.

In some cases, correlating employee performance data with enterprise analytics can give CEOs and CFOs insight into why some organizational leaders deliver better results than others. Coupling well-designed performance management processes with accurate data collection can generate powerful business insights. I worked with one Fortune 100 retail organization that collected detailed data on 448 store managers to examine the impact of their individual performance on organizational results. That quantitative data allowed HR leaders to classify managers as high performing, average, or low performing, and then correlate that information with the financial performance and employee engagement scores of stores they managed.

Analysis of the data provided actionable insights into the differences between managers with low and high performance scores. For example, managers with high performance scores demonstrated 43 percent higher levels of employee engagement in their stores than their low-performing counterparts did.

In addition, high-performing managers experienced 13 percent higher store sales, and those managers were attributable to 32 percent higher store profitability than their counterparts. Using this combination of data allowed the Fortune 100 retailer to directly correlate bottom-line results with the performance level of their employees.[10]

Digging even deeper into the retail data set allowed the organization to evaluate whether or not individual stores needed to improve customer service, drive revenue growth, engage employees, and/or cut costs, with the goal to measure the current leadership team's capability to deliver necessary improvements in those areas. This allowed the retailer to know whether or not it needed to replace leaders who weren't able to deliver results. Executives and HR leaders were so confident in the data, they were able to use it to better leverage the unique talent of their leaders and deliver stronger financial results. While this type of data collection and analysis is no easy undertaking, it is possible (and hugely rewarding) to HR functions intent on impacting financial performance.

Data-driven HR organizations focus on business outcomes, not just on HR outcomes. Studies show that data-driven functions are more likely to be working on maximizing innovation, boosting workforce productivity, and facilitating customer satisfaction with their talent analytics tools than their counterparts. Such initiatives often require using HR analytics in combination with other business intelligence solutions to combine disparate data sources from HR and non-HR environments. Correlating data from HR, finance, and operations, for example, can yield meaningful insights that otherwise might remain undiscovered. The possibilities of data application are endless, but realizing the rewards requires a commitment to building the analytics skill sets in HR, ensuring data integrity, and collaborating well across functions.

Given that CEOs arguably have the largest impact on the financial metrics of a business than any other employee, using highly valid and reliable assessments to evaluate candidates for the CEO job is another crucial task. Chapter 11 details how using a rigorous and multifaceted assessment of CEOs can pay off in improved financial performance of organizations. But this is only possible if the data is trustworthy!

THE ART OF THE POSSIBLE
Realizing the Potential of Talent Analytics

HR leaders who commit to managing talent as strategically as a good CFO manages financial assets seek to improve and expand their use of talent analytics. I believe that these exem-

(continued on next page)

plars explore the "art of the possible" by going beyond efficiency and effectiveness metrics to do the following:

- They develop such a clear understanding of how their
  organizations deliver value (revenue, profit, achievement of
  mission) that they can segment and prioritize which job roles
  in the company are most (and least) crucial to the execution
  of that business strategy.

- They rigorously and accurately evaluate the capabilities of
  people in pivotal roles to understand why some individuals
  deliver more impact to the business than others in similar
  positions.

- They work to understand precisely what motivates high
  performers in pivotal roles, with the understanding that a
  one-size-fits-all approach to motivating key talent often
  guarantees that those individuals will defect to competitors.
  This taxonomy of motivators, or "drivers," includes money,
  which at a certain level has diminishing motivational returns;
  opportunities to learn and grow in job roles or to be promoted; affiliation with coworkers; autonomy, or an ability to
  operate independently of certain oversight; and work-life
  balance. The latter might include providing time to care for
  family, offering sabbaticals, or granting additional vacation
  time so star performers can, for example, surf anytime the
  waves are high.

Once they've determined which roles are pivotal to strategy execution, created an accurate baseline of capabilities for
incumbents in pivotal roles, and identified their engagement
drivers, progressive HR leaders integrate those three data
sources and take action. *Allocation of HR investments of time
and money should start here.* High-performing, high-potential
employees in the most pivotal roles should be paid, developed,
and retained differently from how others in the organization are

paid, developed, and retained. I will provide additional insight on this critical aspect of managing talent in Chapter 9.

Standard salary increases of 2 to 4 percent might now range up to 300 percent depending on an individual's importance to driving competitive advantage. In addition, pivotal employees should receive highly personalized learning opportunities—both formal and on the job—designed to fast-track their development. Efforts to keep them productive and off the competition's payroll also should be highly customized to their individual drivers and desires. Finding new ways to keep these rare individuals engaged and challenged and to keep them producing superior results should be considered a key part of any CHRO's strategic agenda.

The art of the possible is about allocating resources to people and processes in a way that transcends HR's time-honored approach to treating employees as one homogenous group. It requires summoning the courage to move beyond standardization and "extreme fairness" to make tough decisions that have a real impact on bottom-line results. Such an aspiration demands that CHROs and talent leaders demonstrate real conviction and vision about realizing the full potential of the HR discipline.

How Analytics Software Can Help Raise HR's Data Game

The rise of cloud-based technologies, new business intelligence software, and digitized HR functions has created new possibilities to collect and use people analytics in decision making. The venerable HR "data warehouse," long used as the single system of record to analyze metrics like total head count or time to hire, is no longer sufficient to meet modern talent analytics needs.

Today progressive HR functions looking to move beyond basic compliance or operational reporting have digitally powered, integrated software tools that can reveal patterns and trends in workforce data that otherwise wouldn't be apparent at their disposal. These tools include a vast array of analytics for predictive purposes. Rather than having to juggle multiple spreadsheets, HR leaders can now track key workforce performance indicators in easy-to-view, integrated dashboards, drilling down for more detailed analysis where needed.

Despite the growth of these new analytics tools, HR still lags behind other functions in employing business intelligence applications. The most frequently used tool for HR analytics is still Microsoft Excel. One recent industry study reported that 98 percent of organizations use the spreadsheet software for analytics. By comparison, only 40 percent of HR organizations in the study were using a platform business intelligence solution, while 55 percent of respondents were using analytics embedded in human resource management systems (HRMS). Only 14 percent of HR leaders responding to another industry survey reported being "very satisfied" with their current HR analytics technologies.

That's a concern given that today HR data is rarely constrained to human resource technology systems. The discipline of people analytics has moved from a focus on human resource metrics to a focus on the business itself. Leading HR industry vendors have implemented new dashboards designed just for CEOs, for example, to help them better understand data around recruiting metrics, attrition rates, and engagement levels broken out by business unit or manager.

CHROs and HRMS leaders should identify any shortcomings that exist within their data processing and analytics technologies or with the way their systems integrate with other enterprise platforms, and then they need to work to address them.

When asked what they would do to take their talent analytics capabilities to a new level, HRMS leaders responding to a prominent industry survey cited the following desires:[11]

- Increase the use of HR analytics by HR business partners and leaders.
- Report insights beyond operational and compliance reports.

- Blend data from external sources, and in the process help fix the integration problem plaguing much of the IT world today.
- Select metrics and key performance indicators that matter and visualize them through easy-to-use dashboards.
- Leverage data in the cloud to support predictive analytics capabilities.

Amid the hype around analytics software and artificial intelligence, a reminder is also helpful: technology is no end in itself, and the use of cutting-edge analytics tools is no panacea. The latest technology does little to help HR drive competitive advantage if the quality of the underlying workforce data isn't sound or the wrong things are being measured. This is the GIGO principle—again. *CEOs want to know that the right people are being placed in the right roles at the right time to boost profits—while being kept engaged—not how many training classes or performance reviews are completed or what percentage of the workforce is "happy."* Investments in technology should be made with a goal to improve employee performance and measure the right things, not just to gain cost efficiencies.

In Search of Geeks: Building Analytics Competencies on the HR Staff

As CHROs seek to build more data-driven cultures, they also need to rethink the composition of their own staffs. While there is no shortage of skilled recruiters, compliance experts, payroll specialists, or trainers in HR, it is still rare to find employees with advanced statistics, math, or analytics competencies in the function.

Skill sets needed for today's new analytics-driven environment go beyond mere data preparation or quantitative analysis to include critical thinking and effective storytelling. HR needs people with an ability to sift through data to extract actionable insights for CHROs and other senior business leaders. They need people who can think creatively around patterns and data sets. *Generating more data does HR little good without an ability to tell compelling stories from what's being discovered.*

The growing adoption of self-service HR technologies that do things like give employees direct access to their benefits and payroll information is reducing the number of administrative and clerical jobs needed within HR. A report from the U.S. Bureau of Labor Statistics, for example, forecasts that jobs for HR assistant roles will decline by 4.1 percent by 2024. That trend and other resource reallocation decisions may help free up dollars in HR staffing budgets to add more data scientists or technology system analysts to the function.

HR leaders face their own "buy-or-build" decision when it comes to adding analytics competencies to their staffs. Given the dearth of data scientists in the HR field, CHROs and HRMS leaders often must choose between training existing staff in analytics skills and trying to lure analytics specialists from finance, marketing, or R&D departments inside their own organizations. HR leaders also should consider whether these professionals would be better managed in the information technology group.

Regardless of how that staffing choice is made, taking HR's analytics game to a new level will require paying such specialists market-competitive rates and creating an employee value proposition that promises these hard-to-find employees that they will not be signing up to work in a technology "backwater," but will instead have an opportunity to work with the latest technologies, tools, and experts to help elevate HR's standing in the organization.

Review and Action Items

1. HR now has more data than ever, but it's accuracy in predicting business outcomes is highly mixed. HR data quality is lagging far behind that of most other functional areas, and this problem must be addressed.

2. Based on our talent analytics maturity model, HR data today is at "efficiency" level 1. This data is necessary but not sufficient when explaining the impact of people investments on organizational performance.

3. Future people analytics not only will be much higher quality but will also include infinitely faster data collection, as well as exploration of the interaction between data sets to deliver exponentially greater value. Higher levels of insight into an employee's assessed levels of performance and potential combined with insight into his or her engagement drivers will deliver significant improvements in our ability to attract, develop, and retain top talent.

CHAPTER 3

USER EXPERIENCE

Fixing HR's User-Experience Problem: Toward Greater Speed and Simplicity

It's no secret that employees have always loved to hate human resources. As the perceived "police" of employee behavior, the creator of what are often viewed as overly restrictive policies, and the designated bearer of bad news in companies, HR has long been the target of disdain by the workforce.

Whether right or wrong, a perception persists that HR exists to make lives harder for employees and line leaders. While much of that belief is a natural reaction to HR's essential compliance and policing role, some of that negative perception is of the function's own making. If "the customer is always right," and employees are HR's biggest customer, then in many organizations there's something wrong with the way employees are being treated.

The term "user experience" is commonly used in functions like information technology and customer service, where the quality of interactions with technology platforms or service delivery systems plays an outsized role in user satisfaction. An inflexible service policy or insensitive call center representative can ensure that a valued customer never again darkens a company's doorstep. An operating system or software application with slow performance, too many frustrating steps, or lack of modern features will have employees steering clear of that technology and looking for user-friendly work-arounds.

The concept of "user experience" carries less currency in the human resources world. The term itself is used only infrequently by HR professionals to describe their relationship with internal clients, particularly as it pertains to line employees. This may be partially a result of a view that HR exists first and foremost to serve management and secondarily to serve employees. Regardless of the reason, HR has an opportunity to clarify its mission, purpose, and service levels. More clarity on how HR supports both management and employees might keep the disappointment and misunderstandings from surfacing when personal and professional agendas are in conflict.

Employees, leaders, the board, job candidates, and even third-party suppliers are all "clients" of HR, even as it pursues its overarching policing and compliance mission. Much has been written of late about the importance of the "employee experience"; yet on the whole, HR still struggles to effectively engage its stakeholders and consistently deliver real value to them.

Why is this an important issue? Because HR's user-experience problem isn't restricted to the time-honored accusations of having overly bureaucratic policies or inefficient processes or of being too focused on compliance issues at the expense of business strategy. HR has broader user-experience problems that constrain its effectiveness and limit its potential to help organizations execute talent strategies that give them a competitive edge.

To improve the user experience for employees, CHROs must:

- Build more agile functions in tune with fast-moving business needs. HR departments are rarely designed to move with the speed necessary to recruit or develop employees who can support pivoting business strategies.
- Reimagine talent processes like performance management, recruiting, succession management, learning and development, and engagement so they're more "employee-friendly" and less onerous. HR leaders also need to apply people data more efficiently and effectively to improve decision making regarding talent strategy.

- Implement more modern, mobile, and user-friendly human resource technologies that reduce resistance to using HR's services. This can boost adoption rates of HR platforms by the line, improve workforce productivity, and contribute to improved customer service and new labor saving efficiencies in HR shared services operations.
- Avoid adding more complexity to talent management processes and HR service delivery systems. As none other than Albert Einstein said, "*Everything should be made as simple as possible, but not simpler.*" In an era where speed wins, the combination of fast, user-friendly, and competent often captures the day.

Progressive CHROs and talent leaders know that it's only through higher user adoption rates, enhanced employee satisfaction, and more positive word of mouth that they'll begin to remake the oft-maligned HR brand for good. Addressing these chronic user-experience issues—lack of agility in HR operations, unwieldy or provincial technology platforms, and onerous or outdated talent management processes—will go a long way toward helping human resource functions transform how they're perceived within the organization and reposition CHROs as indispensable strategists in the C-suite.

Part 2 of this book will examine in more detail how to apply these user-experience practices to improve processes and outcomes across the talent management spectrum.

The Need for Speed: How to Make HR More Agile

Job roles and talent needs are changing with unprecedented speed in today's organizations to keep pace with disruptive competitors, to support shifts to digital business models, or to drive perpetual innovation. This new reality requires a different type of HR function, one that is far more agile and responsive to shifting conditions and that has an improved ability to anticipate talent needs, instead of just being reactionary.

Changes in business strategy often require high-velocity external recruiting or retraining of existing employees to capitalize on small windows of opportunity; yet most HR functions aren't equipped to help their organizations move like gazelles instead of elephants.

It's one thing to effectively tether talent strategy to business strategy. It's something else altogether to execute quickly enough on talent plans to help your organization stay ahead of competitors. Such "rapid deployment" approaches often require that HR incorporate the agile management techniques common to other disciplines. According to an article in the *Harvard Business Review*, software development teams increasingly find that the fast pace of work they require is hindered by the lack of agility in HR.[1]

Agility requires short development cycles, quick course corrections, and continuous learning, and yet HR too often works in annual or quarterly cycles. The *HBR* article's authors suggest that HR provide the same services it always has, only in ways that are more responsive to the frequent changes in business strategies and work styles of today's organizations. In a recent letter to shareholders, Amazon CEO Jeff Bezos wrote of his efforts to get employees in his maturing company to act as if it's "day 1" of business operations. The alternative—a day 2 mindset—is stasis followed by irrelevance and an inevitable, painful decline. Bezos believes that one of the four essential components of a day 1 strategy is high-velocity decision making.[2]

The ability to make quick decisions at Amazon is made possible by a "disagree-and-commit" system. There will rarely be consensus on any decision, this thinking holds, but it's still possible for those who disagree to move forward toward a goal. Bezos gives the example of being unsure about a proposed Amazon Prime TV series. He writes: "I had a completely different opinion but still wanted to go ahead with it. I wrote back right away with 'I disagree and commit and hope it becomes the most watched thing we've ever made.' Consider how much slower this decision cycle would have been if the team had actually had to convince me rather than simply get my commitment."

One reason that IBM discontinued full-time telecommuting for many of its job roles was to improve the agility and innovation capabilities of its workforce, according to IBM's chief human resources officer Diane Gherson. As IBM's end users require more speed, innovation, and responsiveness in the digital era, IBM's leaders saw a new need for more workforce collaboration at scale. As a result, some 5,000 IBM employees in recruiting, development, design, marketing, and product management who were working from home were asked to return to the office. IBM's belief is that face-to-face communication and on-site work helps to improve continuous innovation.[3]

The company also trained 160,000 employees in agile and design thinking. The result: more IBM employees coming together to cocreate with colleagues, clients, and universities, crossing traditional functional lines to achieve as much as 30 percent quicker time to market on key projects. IBM also said that the move has helped eliminate duplication of effort and reduce decision-making time, *including reducing hiring time in recruitment to 45 days from 85 days for some job roles.*

Forward-thinking organizations are broadening the use of such agile management techniques to areas like recruiting, employee training, and compensation. CHROs with nimble talent strategies often build the recruiting capacity to unearth and lure hard-to-find talent before they, or their competitors, even have job openings.

Here are four examples of how HR functions have acted with greater speed in creating learning and development, recruiting, and compensation strategies to better serve their line clients and support business strategies:

Example 1 Lengthy e-learning courses or weeks-long leadership development programs have increasingly become luxuries as companies look to "skill up" leaders and employees faster to compete in shifting business climates.

Many CHROs and chief learning officers (CLOs) have fashioned new learning and development strategies featuring "microlearning" approaches—content delivered in small, specific segments that are often video based and are designed to equip employees with mission-critical skills or knowledge faster than ever. Such learning is frequently delivered within the flow of work, which avoids having to take employees away from jobs for extended periods for training.

Consider how AT&T used speed as a competitive lever in reskilling its workforce to drive a new strategy tied to wireless technologies and the cloud. AT&T partnered with Georgia Tech University and online education company Udacity to gain immediate access to cutting-edge teaching expertise and content to rapidly retrain these workers for new roles.[4]

As a result, some 140,000 AT&T employees rapidly acquired technical skills for newly created roles right out of the gate, and by the first half of 2016, employees who'd been retrained filled half of all technology management roles in the company.

Example 2   Recruiters who rely too heavily on conventional hiring methods get left behind in today's markets. This is especially true when recruiting hard-to-find technical talent, which can be off the market within 10 days. Recruiting methods need to adapt and become more creative in competitive markets. For example, many quickly growing technology companies make or break their business plans based on how quickly they can find the right software developers, engineers, and salespeople.

Companies undergoing large-scale transformation also have a need for speed. When General Electric began to transform parts of itself into a digital business, the organization quickly lured tech executives from Apple, Google, and Microsoft to help accelerate the change. GE's recruiting leaders also sought to scale up recruitment of software engineers quickly to support a move to cloud-based platforms and an app economy for the industrial sector.[5] First GE hired more recruiters with deep software expertise. Those recruiters used agile methods known as "extreme recruiting" to reduce delivery time of new hires from an average of 10 to 15 weeks to 2 to 5 weeks, offering Silicon Valley levels of compensation to sweeten the deals. In order to attract younger digital talent, GE also rebranded itself, providing more work flexibility and promising top engineers they'd work on meaningful projects that "change how the world works."

Example 3   McDonald's joined the growing ranks of organizations that have migrated away from traditional e-learning courses into more nimble mobile learning and performance support. Frontline employees felt they were learning more from their coworkers than from lengthy e-learning courses, according to Rob Lauber, the chief learning officer at McDonald's. Lauber's team responded by creating a new learning initiative designed to get newly hired employees up to speed faster.

Crew members in McDonald's restaurants now use organization-owned tablets to train directly at 12 core operating stations. These interactive lessons feature both short videos that demonstrate required procedures and graphics-and-text tools that educate employees about restaurant equipment.[6]

Example 4   Rather than relying on the passage of time to gradually close an alarming gender pay gap, executives at Salesforce.com made a preemptive move to close the gap themselves. The company conducted two equal-pay assessments in 2015 and 2017 and found that the pay of both genders needed an adjustment. So CEO Marc Benioff dedicated $6 million to eliminate the pay disparity, paying $3 million in each year with a commitment to continue monitoring the situation for future pay gaps between the genders.[7]

Creating More User-Friendly HR Processes

Agility isn't the only user-experience issue that should be top of mind for talent leaders. Longstanding problems with the usability, efficiency, and strategic nature of some talent management processes continue to impact workforce productivity, limit adoption rates of human resource technology platforms, and taint HR's reputation.

No area of HR has had a historically bigger user-experience problem than performance management. In one recent study 82 percent of companies reported that performance evaluations were not worth their time.[8] Another study found that 41 percent of companies discovered widespread manager bias in their performance reviews.

The way that many organizations conduct work has changed, making it an urgent priority to modernize performance management processes that have been around since the industrial age, for example systems based on once-a-year reviews.

The encouraging news is that many progressive organizations have abandoned annual performance reviews over the past few years and replaced them with more frequent appraisal check-ins. More than 70 percent of companies in a recent global human resource industry study said they were in the midst of reinventing their performance management processes. In some of those cases, companies are disconnecting reviews from annual merit increases.

These organizations have realized that employees want more frequent feedback and meaningful developmental opportunities connected to performance reviews. In this new approach, employee progress against transparent goals is regularly discussed, alignment on what behaviors to start, stop, or continue doing is established, and manager-employee communication—as well as trust—is often enhanced.

We'll take a deeper dive into how to make your own performance management process more user-friendly and agile and better supported by higher-quality data in Chapter 4.

Similar user-experience upgrades could benefit talent processes including recruiting, learning and development, succession management, benefits administration, and employee engagement campaigns. Making talent acquisition processes more "candidate-friendly" reduces the odds that top candidates will steer clear, for fear that your applicant tracking system will send their résumés into a black hole—or that your overly complex job application form will take forever to complete on a phone or tablet. It also creates positive word of mouth about your organization that can spread far and wide on social media.

Progressive organizations understand the value of creating candidate-friendly recruiting processes. Home Depot, for example, recently announced that it will allow some job applicants to self-schedule their in-person interviews.[9] The new scheduling app can be used on any mobile device and is available around the clock. The number of candidates applying to Home Depot increased 50 percent after the app was introduced.

Other companies have redesigned their job application forms so they're far easier to complete on smartphones, and some have implemented new systems that keep candidates better apprised of their hiring status throughout the application process rather than leaving them in the dark.

Rethinking internal recruiting processes and modernizing technology platforms can also make life easier for time-starved recruiters and hiring managers, allowing them to collaborate more effectively and create new efficiencies that help source and hire top candidates faster.

A great example of HR taking very complex processes and making them simple and valuable for end users is at Johnson & Johnson, where the company took a two-day, in-person assessment and collapsed the most highly predictive components and found a way to deliver them virtually, anywhere in the world, on short notice. The company now has actionable data for promotions, external selection decisions, and deep insight into the development needs of more than 1,000 senior leaders. And what do the users think of this process?

- 92 percent of the participants surveyed said the assessment was engaging.
- 89 percent said assessment provided value, focus, and useful strategies for development.

(continued on next page)

- 88 percent of manager responses said the assessment provided value or insight to them.

On the learning and development front, more CLOs and training directors have awoken to the fact that their traditional e-learning courses or instructor-led training programs no longer fit employees' increasingly busy work lives or their preferred learning styles. These learning leaders are turning to new vendor platforms that feature video-based micro-learning, systems that aggregate and curate learning content, and feature mobile-friendly performance support tools that employees can access on the go. This will be discussed further in Chapter 5.

In the employee engagement arena, forward-looking CHROs are realizing that while conducting more frequent "pulse" surveys can be effective in pinpointing often-overlooked factors that make employees disengaged, there's nothing as powerful as the simple (and user-friendly) process of meeting face-to-face with high-performing employees in pivotal roles to conduct engagement "fact-finding" sessions. These high-touch methods are designed to determine the unique factors or "drivers" that keep these essential employees most productive, engaged, and committed at work. Then organizations can pull out the stops to find ways to meet those needs and retain their best employees.

A growing number of HR organizations also have reinvented the way they communicate and administer benefits and other essential human resources information, investing in new self-service, mobile-friendly functions that not only make these processes more employee-friendly; they save HR staff from having to answer or follow up on endless questions.

These highly secure, single sign-on, self-service portals enable employees to view payroll information, time cards, work schedules, vacation accruals, benefits status, and more without having to call or send an e-mail to the HR function. Managers can use their own self-service apps to view or authorize employee shift changes or vacation requests from their phones or tablets, eliminating the previous back-and-forth of calls or e-mails.

Best-in-class employee benefits portals now allow workers to log on to compare benefit plan features, calculate flexible spending options, study insurance coverages, project out-of-pocket health costs, and more. Web-enabled video tutorials or short presentations on these sites help guide employees in making their benefits decisions.

Talent leaders no longer have the luxury of time when it comes to workforce planning or talent management. Operating models and decision-making cycle times have accelerated across the enterprise.

HR also needs to bring a new level of user-friendliness to talent processes if it hopes to boost lagging adoption rates of HR technology platforms, to help take workforce productivity and efficiency to new levels, and to create a perception that HR is as much an advocate for employees as it is for management.

Like their peers in finance, marketing, or operations, HR leaders must become masters of doing things effectively *and* quickly. They also must become as proficient at looking through the organizational windshield as they are its rearview mirror. The ability to accurately predict future recruiting needs or a workforce's shifting learning requirements—and to do so within tight timelines—will separate strategic and highly influential CHROs from their counterparts who are only consumed with compliance or transactional matters.

Review and Action Items

1. The employee user experience in too many organizations is unacceptably poor. HR must take lessons from the consumer world when building applications to support HR processes throughout the talent life cycle.

2. Concepts like "moving with speed and agility" will become an increasingly important differentiator for great HR professionals. Moving with speed to implement new ideas reflective of business and financial savvy will be essential in the HR image makeover.

APPLYING THE PRINCIPLES TO TALENT PROCESSES

CHAPTER 4

PERFORMANCE MANAGEMENT

N othing illustrates what can happen when organizations undertake a determined effort to fix a flawed talent management
process better than the dramatic improvements made of late to
performance management practices. Companies that had reached their
limits of tolerance with this annual rite of appraising employee performance began to cast aside tradition and overhaul what has long been a
flawed and burdensome process.

There is not yet one best practice, but as these changes continue to
evolve, adopting more agile and user-friendly systems that are better
equipped to improve individual and organizational performance has
become a more widespread procedure. Yet if there is a missing link in
this evolution, it's the consistent application of another core principle
espoused in Part 1 of the book—the creation and use of higher-quality
data in making talent decisions. When organizations begin to add more
valid and reliable data to their performance evaluation systems, the process will assuredly take yet another important leap forward.

Moving into the Digital Age

In an interview with a leading human resource industry publication, a
manager for a professional services firm called his company's traditional
performance management process "an investment of 1.8 million hours
across the firm that didn't fit our business needs anymore."[1]

The drawbacks of the traditional performance appraisal process are well documented, with participants on both sides of the interaction expressing chronic grievances. The litany of complaints includes the fact that once-a-year reviews let too much time pass between offering developmental feedback to employees; that annual reviews take an inordinate amount of time and require too much paperwork; that there is too much focus on past performance and not enough on improving future behavior; and that the lack of credible data used in reviews leads to costly compensation decisions and negatively impacts employee morale.

Among the first companies to move their industrial-age models of performance management into the digital age were Adobe, Microsoft, Deloitte, Cisco, and Gap. These organizations abandoned the annual review in favor of systems with more frequent, informal check-ins, the use of near-term rather than annual performance goals, and a stronger focus on coaching and development rather than punitive evaluation. A goal of many of these rebuilt systems is to make performance management *more people-centric and less process-centric.*

According to a recent HR industry study, 70 percent of multinational companies are now in the process of reinventing the performance management process in their organizations.[2]

In this new structure, where check-in conversations occur anywhere from once a week to once a month, managers are able to more rapidly respond to low performance or lagging morale and modify performance goals during the year should team or organizational objectives shift.

The Korn Ferry Hay Group conducted a benchmark study of 10 organizations that were working toward making meaningful change in their performance management design, processes, and practices. Here are some key findings from that study:[3]

- ALL COMPANIES IN THE STUDY HAD CHANGED THEIR APPROACH TO PERFORMANCE MANAGEMENT IN THE PAST SEVERAL YEARS. Half of the organizations were looking for changes in philosophy, including redesigning performance management to support more agile and flexible work cultures. The remainder were focused primarily on improving process efficiencies.

- THERE WAS A DIFFERENCE BETWEEN "IMPROVERS" AND "PIO-NEERS" IN THE STUDY. *Improvers* believe in the fundamentals of their current systems; they seek improvements to their existing processes to make them more user-friendly and to eliminate performance ratings without making other changes. *Pioneers* believe that new models and mindsets are required, are focused on real-time versus annual appraisal cycles, emphasize performance dialogue over ratings, seek to better train managers, and hold managers more accountable for improving their reviews and "unbundling" linkages to rewards.

- THERE WAS A CLEAR TREND IN MOST MARKETS AND REGIONS TO GET RID OF PERFORMANCE MANAGEMENT RATINGS. About 40 percent of peer-group companies in the study were still using some sort of rating to evaluate performance. Among the main arguments for eliminating ratings was the amount of time spent on the calibration and communication process, as well as a feeling of unfairness in the annual appraisal process shared by the majority of employees.

- ORGANIZATIONS THAT HAVE DONE AWAY WITH RATINGS ARE GIVING MANAGERS MORE AUTONOMY AND ACCOUNTABILITY IN THE PROCESS. As a result of this change, companies are increasing the number of informal and formal conversations between managers and employees throughout the year. The idea is to give managers more timely, relevant, and detailed information to ensure that decisions around performance and variable pay are fair and accurate, as well as to provide employees with more frequent feedback about their performance throughout the year.

Companies reinventing their performance management practices also are finding benefits in employee engagement. As managers and employees have more conversations throughout the year, organizations often discover that it improves relationships, creates more trust, and sends a message that managers are invested in their direct reports. One study found that 90 percent of companies that have redesigned their performance appraisals experience improvements in engagement.[4]

One organization well known for innovation studied new employee engagement and was troubled by what it found. Laszlo Bock, former SVP of people operations at Google, found that new graduate hires who didn't understand their job expectations left Google five times more often than those who did.[5] To combat such turnover, Google instituted new expectations related to shared understanding of responsibilities. As reported in *Work Rules!*, Bock said that managers were asked to meet with their new Googlers ("Nooglers") in the first week of employment to discuss three questions:

1. What are your first-quarter objectives and key results (OKRs)?
2. How does your role connect with Google's business goals? Your team's goals?
3. When will your first performance management conversation be, and how will your rating be determined?

CASE STUDY
How One Company Rebuilt Its Appraisal Process

When Deloitte, the global consulting, auditing, and tax firm, launched an initiative to improve strengths-based employee development in the organization, leaders there made an assessment that the company's existing performance management system wasn't aligned with changes that needed to be made.[6]

Focus groups held in the organization found that employees wanted a redesigned performance management system with three key purposes: (1) to better *recognize* performance so it leads to more informed compensation and promotion decisions, (2) to better *see* performance, or to generate a continual stream of higher-quality data that gives managers an improved view into the performance of all employees, and (3) to *fuel* performance with the use of feedback that is more developmental and motivational to take organizational performance to new levels.

Deloitte used that feedback to revamp its performance management system, testing the new process first in small employee populations and then larger ones. The new process features more frequent check-ins and "future-based conversations" about work between managers and employees, with meetings scheduled either weekly or biweekly. No documentation is required going into or out of the meetings to reduce the paperwork burden, participants are given "prompts" to start conversations, and weekly e-mails are sent to see if check-in conversations are being held.

Deloitte also opted to begin capturing performance data in new ways, including use of an evaluation tool called "performance snapshots." Leaders use the tool to assess the performance of team members at certain moments in time, such as at the end of assignments, projects, or milestones, with the goal to capture such feedback at least quarterly. Rather than using traditional ratings to evaluate employees, leaders are asked four questions about employee performance, answered on a Likert-like scale, to help them avoid assessing people too much on their personalities and not enough on their performance.

Performance data from the Snapshot process is aggregated and reviewed quarterly. HR meets with individual line leaders to review their snapshot results, providing an opportunity to discuss any employees who have been identified as low performers, are deemed ready for promotion, and more.

Data Quality Still an Issue

The work of companies like Deloitte to redesign performance management systems is clearly a positive trend. More frequent appraisal discussions mean managers more often are delivering fresh—and thus more credible—feedback rather than struggling to recall events or performance data from months prior.

As business strategies, team goals, and job roles change more frequently in disruptive markets, performance objectives also need to change along with them, making fluid goals more realistic and effective.

But a more modern, agile, strategically aligned, and user-friendly performance management process holds no guarantees of improved data quality. One recent study found that 90 percent of heads of HR still believe their performance management system does not yield accurate information.[7] Tying compensation decisions to flawed talent evaluations can easily cost companies millions (remember, most compensation decisions are tied to flawed performance ratings) and negatively impact employee morale.

Despite the innovations reshaping performance management, too many systems still rely on single managers to rate employee competencies based on a numeric scale, *for example, without rating observed behavior in a way that calibrates measurement across multiple raters.* Holding more frequent performance management discussions has benefits, but the process is compromised if those reviews are based on unreliable data or incomplete talent insights. Most individual managers believe they are above-average raters of others' performance, for example, but the research consistently shows otherwise. Those studies find that most leaders are flawed raters of subordinates' performance, with a list of performance rating errors (idiosyncratic rater effect, just like me, central tendency, primacy/recency) leading to a high rate of poor talent decisions.

New technology is making it easier for managers to do things like "crowdsource" performance reviews, for example, capturing data throughout the year from more people who interact on a regular basis with the employees being reviewed. These kinds of improvements help to avoid the epidemic of subjectivity associated with single-reviewer appraisals.

SUCCESSFUL STORY
Aligning Performance Management
with Business Imperatives

A software company I worked with to improve the quality of its performance management data illustrates how such efforts can pay off in better talent decisions and improved organizational performance. Software implementation consultants in the company were designated as "pivotal" talent because of the vital role they play in ensuring that customers' implementations go smoothly and meet deadlines. A poor implementation can dash the chances that customers will renew their contracts.

The company conducted an analysis to determine the specific performance factors that make their top software implementation consultants so effective. The goal was to identify the "pivot points" that enable these consultants to improve their utilization rates and bill more hours, and then to measure the consultants' performance in those areas more reliably and accurately.

First, the company analyzed how pivot points correlated with consultant utilization rates. Among the most important general competencies characterizing success were "improving processes," "managing work effectively," "sharing information," "creating effective plans," and "thinking broadly." Success in these areas clearly differentiated A-level versus C-level performers.

Next, the company identified more granular behaviors deemed essential to consultant success. Those included "addressing process breakdowns with speed and thoroughness," "identifying ways to streamline and/or improve efficiency of work," and "carefully monitoring the accuracy and quality of work methods and outputs." These behaviors were shown to

(continued on next page)

improve the client's implementation process and increase consultant utilization rates.

The performance analysis ultimately led to a change in
recruitment and selection practices as well as a change in
employee development practices of the implementation consultants. The company began hiring and developing consultants
who possessed more of these A-player, mission-critical competencies, behaviors, drivers, and traits.

Performance management processes used in many organizations are still rife with red tape, another chronic problem that
recent innovations in the processes are beginning to address.
Many organizations still force-fit too many different processes
and decisions into one annual performance management discussion, asking managers to rate employees, document past
performance, make merit increase decisions, and discuss career
development in one prolonged sitting.

In the spirit of user-friendliness, HR leaders should work to
streamline that process and give line managers a chance to
address these important performance evaluation issues in separate stages, not in one soup-to-nuts appraisal meeting.

Technology Upgrades Support Evolution

As performance management systems have evolved, HR technology vendors have modified their own platforms so they're better equipped to support these redesigned processes. Vendors have upgraded performance
management technologies that are part of larger talent management suites
or are stand-alone systems to aid in providing more frequent feedback and
to capture performance data in new ways. Many of these new systems are
now compatible with mobile or social technology interfaces, and some are
designed for use only with work teams, not entire organizations.

The best of these new tools support holding more frequent employee-manager check-ins with features that easily document those discussions and decisions around future development or coaching activities. These platforms also can help manage calibration meetings and handle a variety of compensation models, and some can even initiate feedback events without a manager or employee needing to trigger the action.

Some organizations even have put their own unique stamp on performance management technology by developing in-house apps that gauge what employees should start, stop, or continue doing to improve their performance, with that feedback delivered at more frequent intervals than annual appraisals. These app-based reviews are typically peer-generated—with employees receiving training in how to conduct the evaluations—and can include upward feedback directed to managers. The idea is that an increase in the frequency and quality of data coming from multiple reviewers can lead to more credible appraisal decisions.

Changes to performance management systems will continue to evolve, as pilot tests in organizations eliminate bugs and course corrections are made to this most disliked of HR processes. The welcome news is that the fundamental change in the appraisal format (increasing its frequency) is likely here to stay, in part because that change is being driven as much by business needs as it is by HR imperatives. That combination of drivers should serve as a blueprint for talent leaders as they seek to reimagine other flawed talent management processes in their organizations.

Review and Action Items

1. The traditional end-of-the-year performance review is quickly becoming obsolete. While it does have its pros, there are several alternative approaches that are more appropriate for these changing times. It's best to separate components of the performance management process. Set goals in the beginning of the year, revisit at the beginning and end of big projects or milestones, provide feedback through the

year on a more casual "start, stop, continue" basis. Offer development support and career development advice on a cadence that matches the employee's interest and urgency, and completely remove compensation and succession decisions from the annual review unless the data gathered has been proven to predict business outcomes and in a truly accurate manner, instead of bundled together for review at the end of the year. Important components, including setting goals, providing feedback, paying for performance, and offering job and career development, should be established throughout the year as individual milestones that are aligned with the corporate calendar.

2. While it is still important and relevant to evaluate and differentiate employees and provide wider variation in compensation and development, more accurate and thoughtful methods are encouraged.

CHAPTER 5

LEARNING DEVELOPMENT

Amid the constellation of issues that CHROs and talent leaders oversee, it's easy for learning and development (L&D) to get lost in the shuffle, orbiting beyond the universe of seemingly more pressing, bottom-line matters like managing bonus allocations, recruiting, and retaining pivotal talent.

Indeed, if talent management were a family unit, learning and development would be the middle child, oft-overlooked in favor of siblings. That perception results largely from many organizations still viewing L&D as a luxury, something that is undertaken only in times of robust budgets or to douse the flames of temporary performance problems.

Another school of thought holds that training and development too often competes with the execution of work and that the time people spend on learning is better spent pursuing productivity or revenue goals. After all, shouldn't good recruiting and selection processes make most postemployment learning needs moot?

The reality is that well-conceived and executed development can make the difference between business strategies that flourish and those that languish from lack of proper care and feeding. Consider, for example, the manner in which AT&T transformed its workforce through the use of a highly agile and data-driven learning and development strategy. As detailed in the opening of Chapter 1 on talent strategy, AT&T executives faced a dilemma as their customers began abandoning landlines en masse and switching to mobile devices, forcing the venerable telecom company to undergo a radical digital transformation. The telephone switches and fiber-optic cables that had long formed the backbone of the company were rapidly giving way to the Internet and cloud-based systems.

That disruption created a challenge for executives that went far beyond merely replacing infrastructure. Internal research found that 100,000 of AT&T's workers were in roles the company wouldn't need within a decade.[1] Recruiting externally to close identified gaps in software and engineering talent was deemed impractical given the scale of jobs involved and the relative dearth of outside talent. So AT&T executives launched a billion-dollar employee retraining initiative to drive the change.

AT&T partnered with a respected university and online education company to create a master's degree program in computer science, giving existing employees access to cutting-edge technology content and top instructors to help them retrain for changing roles.[2] The company also launched a new enterprisewide learning portal, created geographic hubs where skills coaches could deliver personalized guidance, and employed apprenticeships to help accelerate learning curves. Those initiatives helped AT&T employees transition from roles like retail sales consultant and billing manager to, for instance, scrum master on software development teams.

The reskilling initiative paid quick dividends. Within a few years, internal candidates had filled more than 40 percent of the 40,000 jobs that had been redesigned to support AT&T's new digital strategy, and more than 140,000 employees have been engaged in some form of retraining to prepare them for future roles.

Learning as a New Strategic Lever

AT&T's retraining initiative could be considered a blueprint for organizations that are undergoing significant change or need to quickly reskill incumbent talent at scale. In today's business environment, where executive teams stand on shifting ground, employees up and down the organizational chart often need to acquire new skills and knowledge faster and more effectively than ever before to support changing business objectives.

This requires HR leaders and chief learning officers to rethink how they build and execute learning strategies from leadership development down to the front lines.

As more executives redesign their organizations to compete in an era of recurring change, the need to rapidly develop or acquire talent for new job roles and skill sets, and to create a pipeline of internal leaders equipped to lead in more volatile and ambiguous business environments, only promises to grow.

One global survey found that 90 percent of CEOs believe their company is facing disruptive change driven by digital technologies; yet 70 percent said their organizations don't have the skills to adapt.[3]

A report from the World Economic Forum found that emerging technologies and socioeconomic forces are expected to disrupt 1.4 million jobs in the United States by 2026. The report analyzed 1,000 different types of jobs, accounting for 96 percent of national employment.[4] The study found that "robust reskilling" will be required to prevent job displacement and declining salaries, with a focus on building highly transferrable or hybrid skills like collaboration, critical thinking, and subject-matter expertise. According to the study's authors, both highly skilled and generalized roles will require this reskilling; otherwise the workforce won't be qualified for the new jobs created by the digital economy.

This new reality requires a reimagining of the legacy learning and development strategies used in many organizations today. CHROs, CLOs, and other learning professionals should consider embracing these new strategic priorities going forward:

1. Develop internal learning plans and external partnerships to reskill existing employees faster and more cost-effectively to support evolving business strategies. As workforce demands continue to outpace employees' skill sets, HR and learning executives will need to become more innovative and agile in how they close talent gaps through learning initiatives.

2. Reevaluate leadership development programs to ensure that rising leaders are being identified and developed with the right types of competencies, experiences, traits, and drivers to lead in more ambiguous, technology-driven, and rapidly shifting environments.

3. Rethink the use of legacy learning technologies like learning management systems (LMSs) to ensure that the right platforms and tools are available to support a growing demand for mobile-friendly "microlearning" and to match how the learning preferences of workers are changing.

Adopting this new agenda will be a challenge for organizations that have been reluctant to look inside their own walls to meet the growing need for workers with contemporary digital skills like data science, software development, or artificial intelligence acumen. Creating such new capabilities in the workforce is only half the battle. Today, that reskilling often must be done at light speed to capitalize on narrowed windows of market opportunity. Traditional operating models across the enterprise need to be sped up, and learning and development is no exception.

Retraining employees as skills grow obsolete or as the need for new competencies arise has become a top priority for CEOs and HR executives. In one survey of those leaders, 83 percent rated the issue of "reinventing learning and careers" as important (second only to the priority of "reorganizing the company for digital business"), and 54 percent rated it urgent.[5] In making the buy-versus-build decision to close talent gaps, executives transforming businesses increasingly find they have to look as much to internal development as they do to external recruiting for answers, particularly when there is a need to do so at scale.

Today's learning and development models are often ill-equipped to address employee development in a way that supports fluid business strategies. Lengthy leadership development programs that are focused only on building generic competencies, for example, or e-learning courses that are disconnected from emerging, real-world work challenges, often do little but create a drag on the P&L by adding low-impact expenses to the income statement.

Companies cannot continue to rely on dated or ineffective development techniques and lose out on valuable opportunities to bring employee skills up to speed as a result. They must be bolder, more resourceful, and accountable when crafting learning strategies that in today's climate have higher stakes and can often make or break the execution of a business strategy.

Forward-thinking CEOs, CHROs, and CLOs are rethinking the way they develop employees at all levels, investing in new teaching methods and technology platforms to create "marketplaces of learning" designed for how time-starved leaders and employees most effectively learn in the digital age. The best of these new models provides a mix of microlearning to fit into busy schedules and longer, macroleadership development programs, tightly connected to strategic objectives.

Rethinking Leadership Development

The recurring patterns of disruptive change experienced by businesses today have significant implications for leadership development programs, initiatives that in many cases are already under siege for a lack of return on investment. For example, when asked to assess the results of leadership development investments in their companies, the majority of 7,500 respondents to a recent Korn Ferry survey rated them only "fair" to "very poor."

A *Harvard Business Review* article dubbed leadership development programs "the great train robbery" for their minimal impact on the performance of leaders and on business results. Citing research from Harvard professor Michael Beer, the article noted that the $162 billion spent in the United States in 2012 on leadership training rarely yielded the kind of return on investment in improved organizational performance sought by companies.[6]

The stakes are clearly high with leadership development investments. Consider that the cost of customized leadership development programs from leading business schools routinely tops $100,000 per individual, and mid-sized and large organizations often allocate vast sums in attempts to develop leaders at varied levels on the organizational chart.

To explore the strategies that companies are using to develop their leaders, Korn Ferry commissioned a comprehensive global survey on leadership development. The survey generated more than 7,500 responses from 107 countries. One of the study's most alarming findings was a growing disparity between the widespread importance of strategic change and the confidence that respondents have that their organization's leaders can deliver that change.

Here are some of the survey's top findings:

- Only 17 percent of those surveyed are confident their organization has the right leadership to deliver on its strategic priorities.
- More than half of executives rank their leadership development ROI as "fair" to "very poor" and would "throw out and rework" half of their current leadership development approaches if they could.
- On average, 50 percent of first-level, mid-level, and high-potential leaders are not active in driving change. Developing leaders to drive strategic change ranked as the highest priority for executives in the survey, and yet nearly half of the respondents reported that managing through strategic change is the number one shortcoming of current leadership.

When top executives don't pay enough attention to leadership development, it can harm the advancement of their direct reports and increase pipeline gaps. This inattention is common due to the day-to-day operational demands and short-term requirements placed on executives. Filling talent gaps, however, is a long-term exercise that should not be overlooked.

One concern among the Korn Ferry survey respondents is that the methods used to develop today's leaders haven't changed to match business climates marked by constant, disruptive change. While executives have always had to reinvent their organizations to keep pace with such disruptions, those changes now arrive faster and in repeated fashion.

When the survey asked business leaders to rank the most pressing strategic business priorities in their organizations, almost half (48 percent) ranked "accelerating the pace of innovation" in their top three out of nine priorities, which was nearly the same as "improving profitability" and "organically increasing market share." This response would have been unlikely 10 years ago.

Future success is determined by a leader's ability to transform his or her organization not just once but on a continuing basis. This type of continued change requires a particular type of executive profile to help organizations prosper. Leadership development is now about more than just developing talent. It's also about helping leaders understand and align on strategy, communication, execution, innovation, change, and growth.

Development initiatives should focus on creating "change leaders" who are excited and passionate about executing business strategy. *If significant time and money is invested in development, then it's reasonable to expect measurable performance or financial improvements driven by participants in the aftermath of development initiatives.*

Leading for change requires a different set of skills than those required for traditional business management. Change leaders must be agile, flexible, and resourceful and have the ability to navigate unknown situations. They also must be good listeners and be open to new ideas from all corners of the organization. And most importantly, the Korn Ferry survey found, change leaders must be able to articulate a vision and inspire others to higher levels of performance.

The reality is that the learning methods used five to ten years ago to address leadership challenges are no longer sufficient. Organizations now need a pipeline of leaders better equipped to adapt to quickly shifting, digitally driven business environments. One way that development initiatives can adapt to this new environment is by moving away from developing a broad variety of general leader competencies to building a smaller set of metacompetencies like learning agility, influence skills, and high-quality decision making. Industry-specific competencies and technical knowledge will always remain valuable, but creating the leader of the future requires rethinking what's necessary to lead successfully in a business landscape that will likely only grow more dependent on tools like artificial intelligence or robotics, and less on people.

The Korn Ferry survey indicated that most leaders preferred development that deals with the contemporary issues they are facing in their organizations over a more abstract, top-down, conceptual approach. Leadership development content should mirror the financial and strategic challenges that a sponsoring organization is facing. It should be grounded in organizational reality and a brisk exchange of ideas, with a focus on what is working well but also where leaders and the organization might be struggling. Development also should lead to fixing the organization's most vexing problems related to customer needs, product challenges, and the best ways employees work together to resolve such issues. Concurrent to solving these business problems, leaders also must be intentional about what they have learned and how they have grown.

As more companies go digital, CHROs and CLOs also need to consider the differences between younger leaders who are "born" into the digital age and internal leaders who are simply adopting digital strategies when building development paths. These two types of leaders often possess different profiles.[7] The "digital natives" typically have deep expertise in specific subject areas, while leaders in traditional firms often have broader skill sets with more experience working across functions. Some born-digital leaders may have a need for greater development in whole-person leadership skills, while those who aren't digital natives could benefit, for example, by action learning projects where they're asked to create a digital platform for inventory management or use technologies like robotic process automation to deliver results more efficiently and cost-effectively.

Timeless Tenets of Leadership Development Success

Rethinking leadership development doesn't mean abandoning its timeless tenets of success. It remains a truism that the most effective programs are *embedded in* business strategy[8] and treated as integral to company success. Respondents to the Korn Ferry survey cited "lack of executive sponsorship" as a chief barrier to successful leadership development practices.

If CEOs and boards don't view leadership development as an indispensable competitive tool, programs won't get the funding, support, or traction they need to thrive. A belief in developing leaders needs to permeate a culture. More organizations also need to think of leadership development as a tool for recruiting the best talent in the market.[9] Effective programs strive to build not only generic competencies but the specific knowledge, skill sets, creative thinking, and resilience needed to lead in today's business environments. High-performing companies understand that the context of a leader's job is fluid; but what they already know matters less than how quickly they can acquire new mindsets or skills.

Well-conceived leadership development avoids the one-size-fits-all syndrome, or the notion that the same set of leadership competencies, behaviors, traits, or drivers is effective regardless of the leader's own development needs, the requirements of the role he or she has, the business strategy, or the company culture.

For example, a company expanding into a new overseas market may need more people with cultural agility and the ability to operate in the local culture, while another may require more diverse leaders to match their changing client demographics. A pharmaceutical company that is moving into digital health solutions may need leaders with specific technical skills, experience with new business models, and innovative mindsets.

Many CEOs also are concerned that they don't have enough leaders in their pipelines to deliver on new strategic priorities. Research from the Corporate Executive Board (CEB) found that 66 percent of companies invest in programs that aim to identify high-potential employees and help them advance; yet only 24 percent of senior executives at those organizations consider the programs to be a success. Only 13 percent of respondents to that CEB survey had confidence in the rising leaders in their firms.

Such results should be considered unacceptable, and the HR function should take a lead role in ensuring that rising leaders are far better prepared to help their organizations succeed in what promises to be an even more tumultuous future. The alternative is watching CFOs or other functional executives reallocate learning and development budgets to investments with higher ROI.

Organizations in the Korn Ferry survey said "filling gaps in the leadership pipeline" was their second most important overall leadership development priority (after "developing leaders to drive strategic change"). When asked to further identify leadership gaps against their business strategy, respondents reported that their top shortfall was having leaders with the "ability to manage through strategic change." This was followed by the desire for "broad and general management capabilities," "specific critical skill sets," and "gender and generational diversity."

The number one gap—finding leaders with "the ability to manage through strategic change"—reflects the growing pressures that organizations face in coping with a rapidly changing economic environment.

What Leadership Development Methods Work Best?

When successful executives are asked about their development as leaders, most don't mention formal learning like classroom training or online coursework. Instead, they cite on-the-job learning experiences. While there can be considerable value in off-site work that allows time for engaging in reflection and exchanging ideas with fellow leaders, action learning projects tied to strategic imperatives give developing leaders the kind of real-world, cross-functional experience critical to leading effectively today.

These projects might include leading a new product launch, developing a new digital strategy, or reviving an overseas unit with lagging sales. Such experiences expose leaders to the daunting challenges and obstacles they'll face as next-level leaders, providing good testing and development grounds for future leadership talent while at the same time often delivering bottom-line payoffs to their organizations.

High-performing companies often use a blended approach to leadership development. "Historically, leadership development has been about one-time events, usually offsite or in classroom settings," says Claudia Hill, global lead for high-potential leadership development at Korn Ferry. "However, research shows that after two weeks only 12 percent of that type of learning is retained and 2 percent applied. Organizations spend money and time, nothing happens, and no meaningful change occurs."

Hill says that leadership development needs to focus on engaging rising leaders on a continuing basis in "big and small ways." That should include a well-conceived blend of workshops, coaching, assessment, peer groups, action learning, technology-delivered learning simulations, immersions, and leaders-as-teachers programs. While more challenging than simply arranging to bring everyone under one roof for lecture-based learning, this blended approach is far more effective, Hill says.

Top programs often use the organization's best leaders as teachers to transfer their experience, hard-won wisdom, and lessons learned to emerging leaders through structured learning, coaching, and mentoring. Learning the latest finance concepts from the CFO after she creatively structured a recent transaction to take advantage of the target's net operating losses, for example, or learning innovative search engine optimization strategies from marketing wizards who have delivered 20-fold increases in site visits or web impressions, adds credibility to training and reduces participant skepticism.

LEADERSHIP DEVELOPMENT
The Whole Is Greater Than the Sum of Its Parts

Specialists can do many things to improve a given talent process, but it's not until selection, performance, succession, and development work together that real strategic lift can be realized. Indeed the whole is greater than the sum of its parts, and

(continued on next page)

there are many pathways and doorways between the different talent processes. Each core process takes on different functions and forms depending on the facet of talent management it is supporting. When tied to *performance management*, for example, development is focused on closing identified job performance gaps in a near-term time period, helping people change behavior to improve current job performance. There is a clear line of sight between what employees are learning and what they are accountable for retaining and using on the job.

When linked to succession management, on the other hand, development becomes more about *readiness* or *potential* to perform. By doing this, organizations give high-potential employees the experience, skills, knowledge, and perspective to help them succeed in future roles. The key difference between readiness and potential is the time horizon. Development pegged to readiness prepares people to take on a new role within a year or two and requires designing and assigning experiences directly relevant to their next job. By using an existing talent architecture, those overseeing development can compare competencies needed for success in a future role against those needed in a current job, then use skill assessments to determine critical skill gaps. Once gaps are identified, developmental events are assigned to begin shoring up or building new skills.

Development tied to *potential* prepares people to assume new positions on a longer time horizon, often two or more years, and encourages them to see their current job responsibilities as building blocks for the future. Such development is inherently more difficult to design, since the period for promotion is unknown and job competencies in future leadership roles are subject to change. Consider the act of preparing a promising middle manager for eventual ascension to an executive role. Giving that manager real-world practice in her current job may not be practical; she may not, for example, have the chance to develop the proper financial acumen for a job that requires managing several divisions, rather than just one department. This manager will need to rotate through other divisions or work on related task forces, shadow others, be mentored by executives, or engage in classroom or e-learning to begin acquiring the skills she needs.

Finally, development also should be tied to the core talent process of selection. This training is usually related to how new hires must perform in their first 100 days. Companies can use the five agendas, outlined here, to create a more focused effort:

- The *business agenda* includes a list of MBOs and the results that need to be accomplished.
- The *learning agenda* details the skills and knowledge that need to be improved to succeed in delivering results.
- The *relationship agenda* outlines which people are critical to success, so that the person can enlist their support early on.
- The *personal agenda* should include the values that are most in line with getting results, along with the objectives that help balance life outside of work.
- The *leadership agenda* outlines the point of view on who a leader is and how he or she will lead others.

Choosing to Build Versus Buy Talent

As the accelerating retirement of baby boomers and the demand for new digital skills create talent gaps across industries, CEOs and CHROs must rethink how they build versus buy talent to execute their talent strategies. For years, organizations could easily fill these gaps with external talent, making the need to retrain existing staff a secondary concern. But as the experience of AT&T demonstrates, the need to digitally transform a business can make a large portion of existing employees' skills obsolete and create a need for new workforce capabilities that aren't easily addressed by recruiting external talent at scale.

If CHROs, CLOs, and CEOs who have skill gaps in their organization are thinking long term, then building talent using learning and development approaches can be the best option. But if talent needs are more urgent, outsourcing a recruiting process to acquire the right talent may be the better choice. The growing use of artificial intelligence, nanotechnology, and robotics also has changed the skills that workers need in the modern economy. According to one study, "skills instability," which refers to the rapid change in skills needed to help organizations succeed, will affect 30 percent of workers in the United States by 2020.[10] Similar studies project a rise in "hybrid" jobs, those positions requiring new combinations of skills. Coding skills, for example, are now increasingly required in jobs outside of information technology, evidenced by the growing number of marketing professionals now asked to develop algorithms.

One reason for the current shortage of software developers, manufacturing workers, and employees with digital skills has been the declining levels of workplace training.[11] Over the past two decades, many organizations in the United States have reduced the amount of training offered to mid-level and frontline workers. A recent report by America's Council of Economic Advisers found that the share of the country's workers receiving either subsidized or on-the-job training has fallen steadily. Increased automation, outsourcing, and use of contract workers convinced many organizations they didn't need to invest in training their full-time employees.

Learning-friendly organizations clearly encourage their people to co-invest in their growth and development. I recall when I joined the HR ranks at AlliedSignal (dba Honeywell), our legendary CEO Larry Bossidy promised to provide at least 40 hours of training to each employee every year. Yet within a few years thereafter, to stress the importance of each employee's personal commitment to his or her own development, we encouraged 40 hours of learning *every week*! Those who took this challenge established personal learning objectives that aligned with their career aspirations. They worked hard each week to learn new things, reflected on new skills, and applied newfound knowledge to their work. Many of these employees were richly rewarded with great careers.

Rise of External Partnerships

Some industries have moved to close their employee training gaps through external partnering approaches. One recent study of learning and development professionals found that 71 percent believe that partnering with outside providers will be the best strategy to get ahead of a widening skills gap.[12]

Healthcare organizations, for example, are addressing a looming talent shortage by using such partnerships to reskill existing employees. According to the U.S. Bureau of Labor Statistics, the industry will experience a shortfall of primary care physicians, nurses, specialists in anesthesiology and radiology, and support staff in the coming years, with nearly half of all registered nurses reaching retirement age by 2020. HR leaders and CLOs in healthcare have found that coordinating with universities, government agencies, and workforce development entities to reeducate existing staff or students for these high-demand job roles can help resolve staffing challenges. These development approaches include internships, registered apprenticeships, externships, and the creation of "in-house-talent incubators." Geisinger Health, for example, launched an internal training program in partnership with a local college to help create more certified medical coders. Rather than trying to recruit these specialists from a limited external talent pool, Geisinger offered current employees who were interested in becoming coders an opportunity to be trained and certified.[13]

Lowe's, the chain of home improvement and hardware stores, created a new workforce training program called "Track to the Trades" to address a growing skills gap in the organization. The program gives employees financial assistance to become certified in certain trade skills like heating and air conditioning, electrical, plumbing, carpentry, and appliance repair. Employees who qualify for the program can receive up to $2,500 to complete their education through a partnership with Guild Education.[14]

The program is designed to build a pipeline for the next generation of skilled trade workers in the company.

As companies continue to find new applications for artificial intelligence and machine learning, CHROs and talent acquisition leaders also find themselves with a pressing need for talent in those areas. To address the talent gap, companies like Google and Facebook have begun offering on-site classes in AI techniques for engineers and other incumbent employees.[15] Fields like AI and cybersecurity often evolve faster than degree programs can adapt, forcing companies to create talent pools themselves if they want to develop or find the talent they need. Some employers have turned to IT "boot camp" classes or digital credentialing to meet the acute need for certain skills.

Studies also show that more organizations are moving toward *skills-based hiring* and away from hiring based primarily on educational backgrounds. One survey found that 60 percent of companies said they'll start choosing candidates primarily based on what they can do, rather than on a "degree or pedigree," suggesting an increase in the use of skill assessments to evaluate skills.[16]

REQUIEM FOR THE LMS
A New Era Dawns for Learning Technologies

The emergence of new technology platforms is making it possible for chief learning officers to deliver learning to the enterprise in more agile and impactful ways. For years, the venerable learning management system has been the centerpiece of corporate learning, a platform designed with the chief purpose of tracking an organization's instructor-led and online learning, primarily in the areas of compliance and regulatory training.

But the LMS has gradually been pushed to the periphery in many companies, as industry vendors have introduced new systems for digital learning, platforms that are content-rich and mobile-friendly and better suited to how employees prefer to learn today. While the LMS will continue to be important for compliance management, certification pathing, tracking of learning credits, etc., it will no longer be the nerve center for corporate learning.

The growing popularity of video-based microlearning through YouTube-like learning channels, the growth of user-generated training content, and the emergence of tools like massive open online courses (MOOCs) have paved the way for new types of learning technologies. As the number of learning options available to employees outside the organization has mushroomed—videos, podcasts, expert blogs, webcasts, articles, and the like—CLOs have begun replicating that model in-house, hoping to deliver more consumerlike learning experiences.

In addition to usability issues, one chronic problem with LMS platforms has been the limited amount of learning content they make available to the workforce. When respondents to a recent industry survey were asked which additional vendors besides their LMS played a key role in rounding out a learning environment, content providers topped the list. Vendors that offered microlearning courses, collaboration tools, content management, and regulatory programs were all viewed as critical.[17]

More CLOs also are crafting learning strategies with the understanding that workers have less time than ever before to learn while on the job. Some research shows that the average employee has only 25 minutes a week to set aside for learning.[18] That reality has fueled the rise of vendors who specialize in microlearning solutions or who aggregate and curate content to save employees time. Rather than offering long, page-turning e-learning courses, these vendors provide "learning on

(continued on next page)

demand" with content that takes 15 minutes or less to consume and can be accessed when needed.

Authoring video-based learning content has also become easier and more affordable than ever before, allowing subject-matter experts in companies to partner with instructional designers to build educational videos without the need for expensive equipment or dedicated studios. Industry vendors have built capabilities that enable easy management and distribution of videos inside companies into their platforms.

For deeper learning needs that require more of an employee's time, other established vendors now offer learning tools like MOOCs, longer courses featuring a series of video-based modules or instructor-led online programs typified by group discussion, simulations, and more.

Many of these new learning platforms also feature artificial intelligence and machine learning capabilities that can recommend learning activities to users based on assessments, preferred learning styles, past experience, or career development goals. The best of these systems leverage the latest analytics tools to personalize learning to employees' distinct needs.

Measuring the Impact of Learning and Development

Two additional issues continue to undermine the ability of learning and development to effectively drive business strategies. One is a propensity to fund new training initiatives without sound evidence that learning is the best solution to a performance problem. In a common scenario, a line leader approaches a CLO or training director with an urgent request for a new training course to solve a problem with slowing sales, a rise in customer service complaints, poor teamwork, or other performance issues. All too often, formal learning programs for those requests are approved without further investigation into whether a lack of skill or knowledge is causing the problem. In some cases, inadequate resourcing, poorly designed systems, or worker motivation is the cause of the issue, not a lack of education. For example, employees might already know what to do but are not doing it. They may not understand what's expected of them, they may not have the right tools to properly execute the job, or compensation structures and recognition practices may not be supporting desired performance.

A performance analysis would unearth that root cause, but in the rush to fix the problem, that step is often viewed as too complex, and training is pushed through instead. The predictable outcome is delivery of a costly learning program that does little to address underlying performance issues and casts further doubt on the ability of learning professionals to deliver value to the organization.

The second issue is a continuing reluctance to measure the impact of leadership development programs on individual and organizational performance. Too often CEOs or other senior leaders evaluating the performance of CLOs are content to let participant feedback be the only gauge of whether programs had a significant impact—the "smile" sheets that simply measure whether leaders liked or disliked the program.

Only 15 percent of talent development professionals measure the ROI of any learning programs, according to a recent report from the Association of Talent Development. Another survey from the *Chief Learning Officer* business intelligence board found that only 50 percent of respondents attempt to measure learning's impact on business performance, and even fewer (36 percent) extend the effort to specific results like sales.

Conversely, 93 percent of learning organizations in the *Chief Learning Officer* study measure employee *response* to training—the smile-sheet approach commonly known as level 1 evaluation in the Donald Kirkpatrick model. The study included responses from 1,500 professionals in the learning and development industry.[19]

Why this continuing—and alarming—lack of measurement rigor? Reasons run from learning organizations lacking analytics expertise, to limited dollars for conducting ROI studies, to the C-suite not holding the CLO's feet to the fire to prove strong ROI. Research from the *Chief Learning Officer* business intelligence board found that only 14 percent of learning organizations say they have the right technology needed to collect, integrate, and analyze data from across multiple HR systems. Such technology is critical in this era of big data. The good news is that 70 percent of learning organizations in the study planned to increase their analytics capacity in the coming years.

Now more than ever, companies need to ensure that their high-stakes investments in learning are paying dividends. Quickly and capably reskilling incumbent employees for new roles and responsibilities that are connected to shifting business strategies is a necessity that will only become more and more prominent. In an article titled "So Much Training, So Little to Show for It," the *Wall Street Journal* found that without meaningful assessment or practical follow-up, 90 percent of newly learned skills are lost within a year.[20] *What happens before and after learning sessions, the article asserts, is just as important as the actual instruction itself.*

Organizations should attempt to evaluate the impact of learning programs on personal behavior as well as on organizational results, particularly for initiatives deemed essential to strategic objectives. That could include the use of tools like 360-degree feedback at the beginning of a leadership development program and again six months or a year later to evaluate behavioral change in leaders who completed training.

It's important that 360 tools are used wisely, however, paying close attention to how survey questions are phrased. The best questions compare learners' posttraining performance to pretraining levels; and for each targeted learning objective, raters should evaluate the behavior of the leaders relative to their performance six months ago. Are they (a) worse, (b) about the same, or (c) better?

Insight from these questions helps leaders create a list of behaviors to stop, start, or continue doing to improve their future performance. Open-ended comments can also serve as an exclamation point on numerical ratings and provide color commentary on specific areas for improvement.

Some organizations evaluate the impact of leadership development on the business by comparing the average productivity of participants' teams before and after a training program.[21] Others look to measure revenue increases or other improvements—such as a leader's career progression, performance rating, or turnover on their teams—by comparing groups who received leadership training and those who didn't.

Some shy away from measuring the impact of leadership development beyond level 1 participant feedback because they believe it adds significant costs to the effort. Yet one study found those costs to be low considering the potential benefits of effective leadership programs to business results.[22] For high-stakes programs tied to driving business strategy, an investment of 5 to 10 percent of program costs to demonstrate ROI represents a minimal expenditure.

As the need grows for new types of learning content, delivery strategies, and measurement approaches, HR leaders and CLOs should adopt a new strategic agenda moving forward. Success will require a focus on these key areas:

- Precisely identify the core needs of learners, using contemporary needs analysis methods.
- Procure more content relevant to real-world needs and adopt modern, user-friendly learning technologies to close talent gaps with greater speed and to address employees' changing learning preferences.
- Incorporate the crucial opportunity to practice new skills on the job and deliver expected results from challenging experiential exercises into leadership development strategies.
- Be accountable for demonstrating the impact of learning expenditures on performance with either quantitative metrics or impactful qualitative evidence, stories, and commentary.

Review and Action Items

1. Well over $100 billion is spent on leadership training per year, and yet the return on investment is extremely hard to measure. In order for investments to continue, much stronger ties to business impact must be established.

2. Classroom learning experiences may help build culture or camaraderie among attendees, but this method is not as effective as asynchronous, blended, or on-the-job methods. Mobile and remote learning trends will continue to increase as well.

3. Assessment of job performance to identify pivot points critical to success and measures of learning agility and preferred learning style are recommended when improving efficiency and effectiveness of learning and performance. These approaches require tighter integration of HR subsystems: performance management, learning, and succession planning among others.

CHAPTER 6

SUCCESSION PLANNING

The most important step that talent leaders can take to ensure the future health of their organizations is to build strong leadership bench strength in their ranks. While few CHROs would argue with the notion that succession planning should be a strategic, data-driven, and highly agile process, many organizations still fail to apply those three core principles—the pillars of this book—to their succession management processes.

The ongoing epidemic of promoting the wrong leaders into mission-critical jobs cripples revenues and profits and proves toxic to employee morale. For leaders who are wrongly promoted into next-level jobs, poor decisions can derail or even end their careers.

A global research study by Korn Ferry found that *only one-third* of respondents were satisfied with the outcomes of their executive succession programs. The survey covered 54 countries globally and companies ranging in size from 500 to 50,000 employees, generating more than 1,000 responses from business leaders in the C-suite as well as executive and director levels.[1] In addition, in Deloitte's "Global Human Capital Trends" study, 30 percent of organizations reported they had "weak" or "very weak" leadership pipelines, with 90 percent of those organizations viewing the problem as a "critical challenge."[2]

The reasons that companies offer for not getting around to succession planning are invariably long. HR and senior leaders are consumed with near-term responsibilities, and finding time for longer-term planning like succession management is a challenge. In other cases, an assumption exists that the "next in line" will naturally ascend to leadership roles upon a resignation, transfer, or firing. Finally, there can be resistance in the C-suite from top executives hesitant to acknowledge the reality that they'll one day leave the company and need to be replaced.

But high-performing organizations resist such excuses and make succession planning an indispensable part of their strategic plans. Talent leaders in these companies apply the core concepts of strategic thinking, rigorous assessment, and process agility to make succession planning a linchpin of talent strategies. They recognize that critical leadership and management roles exist at all levels of the company, not just in the C-suite, and work diligently to build multilevel succession plans that ensure that capable leaders are always waiting in the wings.

According to the Korn Ferry succession management study, there remains a disconnect between succession plans and business strategy, despite the investments that organizations have made in succession management in the last 20 years. But the companies that win are those that strategically align their succession plans with the direction of the business. Their plans identify candidates who can change quickly and have the learning agility to move as the target moves for the business's success. (We discussed this critical step in Chapter 1.) High-performing companies know that it's important to keep succession plans nimble and flexible. They understand that in a world where cycles of disruptive change grow ever shorter, leadership requirements can change quickly and succession plans must change along with them.

Good succession plans provide key intelligence on pivotal roles, recognize the business impact of vacancies, specify the traits and drivers of top-promotion candidates, and identify where the most potentially damaging talent gaps lie. This succession insight is key to identifying, developing, and successfully promoting a steady pipeline of "ready-now" leaders.

Where Succession Management Goes Wrong

Where are organizations going wrong with succession planning? Here are the key problem areas identified in the Korn Ferry survey:[3]

- LACK OF CONFIDENCE IN IDENTIFYING POTENTIAL. Only half of respondents (51 percent) feel that their organization has accurately pinpointed the potential future leaders they should be investing in.
- NOT TAKING A WHOLE-PERSON VIEW. Almost two-thirds of respondents in the survey (63 percent) said that a lack of *well-suited traits and dispositions,* not competencies or skills, is the biggest cause for concern in failed promotions.
- IGNORING THE COMPLETE TALENT PIPELINE. Organizations typically only include 13 percent of skilled professionals and 38 percent of mid-level managers in succession management programs. That incomplete picture of the talent pipeline leads to overlooking emerging managers with next-level potential, and it sends a signal to those managers that they may not have a future in the company. Companies must look at the complete leadership pipeline to create a sustainable, consistent flow of leaders.
- TOO MUCH TALENT "BOUGHT" AND NOT ENOUGH "BUILT." Most survey respondents agreed that a 2:1 ratio of "build" versus "buy" is preferred, but the majority still end up going outside more often than they would like to when obtaining talent.

Failed promotions and bad hires can cause significant losses in productivity, impact morale, and cause negative impressions and disengagement, resulting in huge financial costs to the organization. The top three risks of ineffective or absent succession plans identified by survey respondents were (1) losing ready-now internal candidates, (2) alienating potential successors, and (3) naming an ill-fit successor. These issues were closely followed by impacts on employee morale, workforce turnover, and competitive decline.

Not only must CHROs and other talent executives have a deep understanding of whether selected high potentials are ready for that next promotion; they should also be confident that those individuals will be successful in significantly more challenging roles. To ensure that, organizations must look beyond past performance to understand the *leadership traits and drivers* critical to success in next-level leadership roles.

Flawed succession management practices do more than just put businesses at risk. Many careers have been ruined when the wrong person is promoted into the wrong job. Too often poor succession practices result in huge costs, loss of a strong performer in a current role, and the addition of a leader who isn't ready for a new role. The predictable outcome is a major disruption not just to the business but to the newly promoted leader and his or her family.

PERFORMANCE VERSUS POTENTIAL
How Misconceptions Lead to Promotion Failures

While it's a truism to say that most high potentials are high performers, it doesn't always follow that performance is the only indicator of potential. For succession planning to succeed, organizations must start by accurately identifying *high-potential* talent early in the succession management process.

In the Korn Ferry succession management study, survey respondents ranked *compatible skills and competencies* as the main drivers behind their promotion decisions, closely followed by well-suited traits and dispositions.[4] Prioritizing in that fashion suggests that too many organizations still promote primarily on *performance*, without looking beyond today's success and considering how well candidates will fare in significantly more challenging roles.

Understanding the distinction between *performance* and *potential* is vital to making good succession decisions.

Performance looks at how effective someone is in his or her current role and only *reasonably predicts* success in similar types of roles—and only if the individual alone was primarily responsible for past success. When measuring performance, companies should assess for competencies, results, and achievements in the current role.

Potential, on the other hand, is a measure of a person's future capacity to be effective in a significantly more challenging role while applying lessons from previous experiences. When assessing potential, organizations need to measure experiences, traits, and drivers that demonstrate the *motivation and interest* to succeed in more complex, senior roles. Measuring compatible skills and competencies here isn't sufficient.

Each leadership level requires different capabilities, traits, and drivers (see Figure 6.1). Being promotable or ready for that next job is about having the ability to develop the qualifications needed for bigger, more complex positions further down the road. Identifying those key leadership traits and dispositions early in a person's career, be it learning agility, emotional intelligence, drive to succeed, resilience, or ability to deal with ambiguity, is a key step to ensuring the success of promotions.

FIGURE 6.1 The changing requirements of leadership

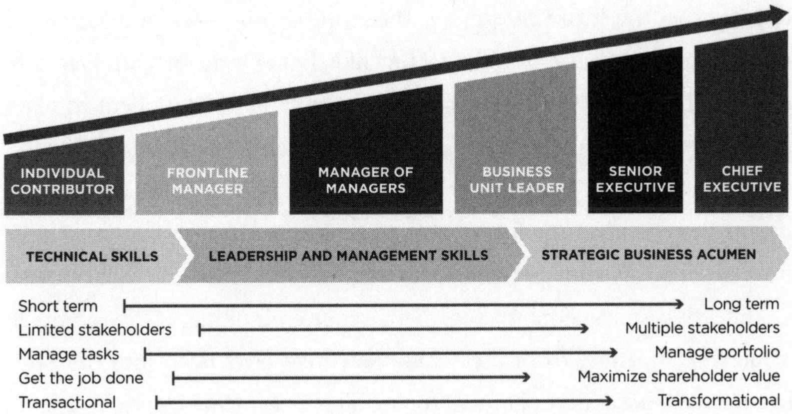

As the survey findings reveal, executives rate compatible skills and competencies as the most significant qualities for driving promotion decisions; however, *the number one reason*

(continued on next page)

promotions fail is due to unsuitable traits and dispositions.[5] In other words, people are often hired because of "whom they know" but are fired for "who they are." Traits and dispositions frequently get overlooked when considering a manager's true potential for advanced leadership, and lead to the all too common *promote-to-failure* syndrome.

A multidimensional leadership analysis is vital in improving the success of leadership promotions. Talent leaders and senior executives must embrace this whole-person perspective, or the chances of identifying the wrong talent increases, which can not only hurt the individual but negatively impact the business for years.

Planning for the Entire Talent Pipeline

In today's business environment, it's important to identify and develop talent across the entire enterprise. The scope of jobs is widening, new job roles are emerging as a result of factors like digital transformation and the growth of artificial intelligence, and the supply of pivotal talent in many fields is getting smaller. Talent is also being promoted to senior management much earlier than it was in the past at many organizations. That means there is less time for up-and-coming executives to become "ready now" than at any time in the recent past.

Effective succession management requires looking at the complete leadership pipeline, from the senior executive level deep into the organization. A succession plan will look different for lower levels of leadership, but HR leaders will still be able to find valuable talent there that they can help groom and invest in as eventual successors. Companies need to start identifying and developing talent further down the pipeline—simply looking at the top of the org chart for future leaders is no longer a viable option. Korn Ferry's survey found that many companies are not reaching far enough down or starting soon enough in identifying potential candidates to create a supply of ready leaders.

Early-career employees who might be considered for broader leadership roles longer-term need to be identified early so they'll have time to develop and be ready when the time comes. To ensure proper identification of early career employees worthy of differentially high investment requires an assessment of potential to be future leaders. Such assessments should also leverage the latest technologies and artificial intelligence for high-volume, low-cost solutions to identifying early-career leaders worthy of investment. The insights delivered by these new tools can be powerful predictors of future success and provide "developmentally actionable" analytics.

Many organizations fail to strike the proper balance of investment between high-potential leaders and the "vital many," which includes *high-professional talent*. High-professional talent are those with skills and expertise essential to the success of the business, but who are often overlooked in companies for leadership advancement. These professionals can be difficult to replace because they are usually industry experts with a wealth of organization-specific knowledge.

The fact that only 13 percent of survey respondents in the Korn Ferry study included skilled professionals in their succession management planning—those often referred to as high-professional talent—is indicative of a need to consider broader leadership pipelines in succession plans.

THE SEVEN SIGNPOSTS

A Framework for Measuring Superior Leadership Potential

In order to accurately identify those who will be successful in next-level leadership roles, it's imperative for organizations to have a complete talent picture of the whole person, not just a

(continued on next page)

snapshot of today's job performance. The "signposts," shown in Figure 6.2 and described below, refine the indicators of high potential for leadership into seven categories. All these signposts can be precisely measured and quantified, enabling organizations to predict with a high degree of accuracy which leaders have the greatest likelihood of succeeding once promoted.

FIGURE 6.2   The seven signposts

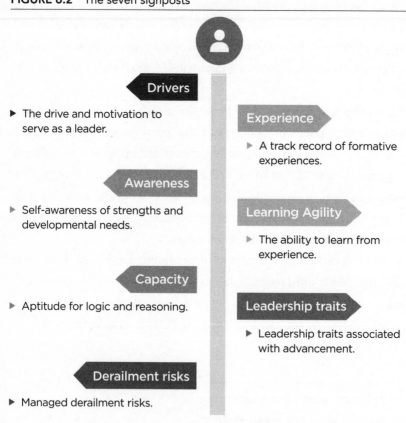

1. LEARNING AGILITY. This is the ability and willingness to learn from experience and apply that learning to perform successfully under new or first-time conditions. With only around 15 percent of the workforce considered to be highly "learning agile," identifying this natural aptitude early on is

critical to pinpoint the leaders who will excel in future roles. According to Korn Ferry research, companies with the greatest rates of highly learning-agile executives deliver 25 percent higher profit margins compared with peer companies.

2. A track record of formative EXPERIENCES. These experiences prepare a person for future leadership roles. Examples are developing strategies, participating in critical negotiations, working across different functions and geographies, and running start-ups, turnaround situations, and mature businesses.

3. SELF-AWARENESS. This refers to the ability of individuals to know their strengths in addition to their development needs. These employees often seek feedback on ways to improve and reflect on their own successes.

4. LEADERSHIP TRAITS. These are inclinations and aptitudes, such as assertiveness and tolerance of ambiguity. Traits can assume greater or lesser importance at higher leadership levels.

5. "FIRE IN THE BELLY" TO BE A SENIOR LEADER. Individuals who aspire to become senior executives relish the challenge of taking on more responsibility. They will actively seek out leadership opportunities, often citing the nature of the work as their primary motivator.

6. APTITUDE FOR LOGIC AND REASONING. The demonstration of analytical and conceptual abilities leads to using logic and pursuing sound strategic choices.

7. MANAGED DERAILMENT RISKS. The risks of derailment increase at higher leadership levels. Leaders need to be aware of their unique derailment risks, which could be anything from micromanagement and intimidating behavior to passive-aggressive actions. Unless leaders learn how to effectively manage these tendencies, their careers in management can be cut short.

Importance of Transparency

Creating a *transparent* succession management process is critical not only to retaining and engaging high potentials but also to fostering other key talent in the organization. If promising individuals don't understand their career prospects, they are at a higher risk of leaving, which can impact overall employee morale as well as result in the loss of a potentially effective leader. Yet most organizations avoid communicating career potential to their people.

The Korn Ferry survey revealed that directors and those at lower managerial levels were the most dissatisfied with their organization's succession outcomes. Put yourself in the place of an ambitious mid-level leader with potential and a strong track record of success. No one has approached you to talk about your future. You are likely to become disengaged, and most high potentials who have a good sense of their talent and market opportunities will get impatient and leave an organization that ignores them.

Organizations need to communicate expectations for high-potential employees and key roles, providing resources for development so that these employees have the opportunity to enhance their skill sets, even if they don't have the potential to advance to the very top. The alternative is to risk losing your best people.

Most companies concentrate succession plans on their high potentials, but the reality is that these employees are only a small percentage of the workforce. Companies should clearly communicate with all employees so they understand what is needed to enhance their contribution to the organization and realize their career aspirations.

Making the Build-Versus-Buy Decision

Korn Ferry's research finds that most organizations clearly favor build (developing leaders from within) over buy (hiring outside) in their succession management decisions.[6] Yet when sourcing leadership talent, almost half of survey respondents said they were more dependent on out-side hires than internal promotions.

So what is the right mix of build versus buy?

There are obvious advantages to internal promotion. It ensures a deep, thorough understanding of the organization, allowing business intelligence to be passed along to the next leader. It enables companies to build the skill sets and leadership styles that meet their precise needs. It also helps with attraction of top, mid-, and lower-level talent from outside the organization by demonstrating that the company is committed to growing leaders.

There will, however, be situations where organizations have to rely on external hires. Examples are start-ups, companies in emerging industries, and organizations that are experiencing rapid growth but haven't been able to develop the necessary talent fast enough.

There also can be unique benefits to sourcing candidates outside the business when seeking to grow faster than a current workforce can handle, when infusing new thinking and driving change, or when there is a need to design and execute new business strategies.

Ultimately every organization's build-versus-buy mix should reflect its specific needs and maturity level. The more well conceived the succession plan, the more likely the organization is to realize its potential and over-come setbacks.

MEASURING READINESS
What Does "Ready Now" Really Mean?

Having a steady stream of global ready-now leaders is the ultimate goal of any succession management plan. However, the Korn Ferry succession management study found that half of all respondents don't feel that their organization has a sufficient ready-now talent pipeline.

(continued on next page)

Developing leaders who can be officially deemed *ready now* takes consistency, accountability, and a systemic approach. This can be challenging for organizations that don't have an effective, continually refreshed succession management plan and (often because of the absence of quality people data) lack a clear picture of the current state of their talent's true readiness.

It's common for such organizations to struggle with leaders who have been on a succession chart for years and whose development lags as a result. Likewise, when a position opens, it can often go to a candidate who is not on the succession chart, creating disruption not only to the business but to teams, culture, and morale.

It's critical for talent leaders to develop a nuanced picture of how candidates need to be developed to succeed in next-level roles. Stu Crandell, senior vice president, Board & CEO Services at Korn Ferry, notes: "How can you ever be 'ready now' if you don't know what you are supposed to be ready for? The disconnect keeps people in a perpetual state of development no-man's land."

There should be a granular level of specificity about the skills and experiences needed to succeed at the next leadership level. Is it cross-functional experience that includes supply chain or R&D management? Delivering against aggressive revenue growth targets in emerging markets? Successfully integrating an acquisition so that revenue and cost synergies exceed the targets committed to the board and shareholders? The more specific the role profile, the better when evaluating candidates and then using identified gaps to prepare leaders for next-level jobs.

How can an organization accurately determine readiness for promotion? After a period of development, you can assess leaders to see how they will perform against the challenges of a more advanced role. Typically, these assessments are live simulations that create the unique pressurized environment and decision-making scenarios that the leader will face on the job. Simulated assessments show a leader's current state of readiness and also give the leader being tested a realistic snapshot of what an elevated role will feel like. At Korn Ferry we simulate a year's worth of challenges in a single day, and we deliver these assessments all over the world to meet client demand.

Figure 6.3 presents data from the previously cited succession study.[7] It reveals that although ready-now candidates consistently produce good business results a majority of the time, few organizations currently have a solid pipeline of ready-now leadership candidates.

FIGURE 6.3 Results of survey questions

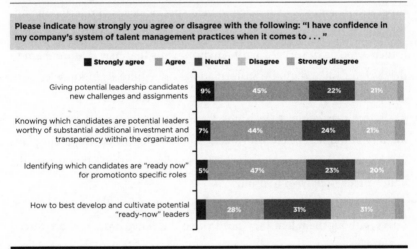

Targeted Development Is Key

Why is there such a shortage of strong leadership bench strength within many organizations? One reason is because leadership development strategies in too many companies are producing leaders with generic, "lowest-common-denominator" skill sets and then expecting them to take on very specific challenges of a new and differentiated strategy. Development needs to be inextricably linked to current business challenges, an issue addressed in more detail in Chapter 5 on reinventing leadership development.

Only 54 percent of respondents to the Korn Ferry survey felt that their organization was providing potential leadership candidates with valuable new challenges and assignments tied to driving strategy.[8] These very vital experiences of developing successful leaders must be intentional and gained over time. Every organization needs to define which experiences are critical for success in a job role or level, and senior leaders should have input in creating these development experiences and opportunities for rising leaders. These experiences should be *diverse, intense, varied*, and *adverse* (DIVA). Examples could include dealing with turnaround and start-up situations and gaining cross-cultural or international experience.

Leaders too often spend time participating in standard development programs that aren't customized to their specific needs, hindering the fulfillment of their true potential and depriving the organization of future leaders capable of succeeding in environments that may require them to drive change like digital transformations or acquire deep knowledge of competitive tools like artificial intelligence and robotics.

Before development decisions are made, it's important to accurately identify and differentiate your talent so that effective development plans can be created and implemented. This requires a culture that values the ability of all employees to grow.

Organizations that don't start development early will often find themselves without the talent they need when the time comes and are forced to scramble frantically to fill open spots from outside the company, sometimes from shallow talent pools.

To be truly effective, succession management across the organization must accurately map the supply of talent against demand, tying that process to current and future business goals. Plans must be aligned with business strategy to link a definition of what kind of talent is needed to the sometimes-shifting direction of the organization. Taking a holistic view across the entire leadership pipeline will enable HR leaders to include the valuable talent that often resides at lower leadership layers.

Ultimately it comes back to the three-step succession planning "waltz." Organizations need to understand the talent they require for future growth, benchmark this against the talent they have, and then work wisely and diligently to close those gaps.

Review and Action Items

1. Succession planning is a mandatory board and executive team business process. Both spectacular failures and successes make clear the necessity of proactive leadership pipeline procurement.

2. A framework of essential succession process steps is proposed. Defining an organization's unique talent demands is first; taking inventory of pipeline performance, potential, readiness, and fit using predictively powerful tools is next; finally, closing individual, team, and organizational gaps is last. Methods for each step are reviewed.

3. The importance of measuring the whole person is discussed, seven signposts of leadership success are detailed, and methods for gathering externally benchmarked data across the entire pipeline are shared.

For more insight on succession for CEOs, refer to Chapter 11 on boards of directors.

CHAPTER 7

COMPENSATION

I t's well known that employee compensation accounts for one of an organization's most significant investments. Depending on the industry, compensation costs can range anywhere from 30 to 70 percent of an organization's total expenses. Given the size of that investment, it stands to reason that reward professionals would be among the most strategic, creative, and analytical leaders in the HR space as it relates to rewarding, retaining, and engaging top talent in support of business strategy. While that may be the case in some high-performing organizations, the reality is that reward leaders of this kind are in the minority. Most are taught and encouraged to act conservatively, to compensate all employees equally, to be even-handed in their practices, and to mitigate risk.

That conservatism can be good when it comes to compliance issues and a need to control growth in employee expenses. But overly rigid compensation philosophies become an obstacle when attempting to pay, reward, and retain pivotal employees in ways commensurate with their disproportionate impact on an organization.

Linking Compensation Strategies to Pivotal Talent

HR has a clear need for more strategic and creative thinkers in the compensation arena. Job one for these professionals should be to work backward from a deep understanding of how organizations make money (keep shareholders happy) and, as well, to understand which roles are the most pivotal to organizational success. As we discussed in Chapter 2, the relative impact that one role may have on company performance versus another is dependent on the unique strategy of the business.

Once a clear link between strategy and the value of job roles is established, high-quality analytics are needed to understand the true value of these roles to the organization. Reliable and timely data is also necessary to establish a baseline measure of the performance and potential of incumbents in these pivotal roles. With those key factors established, CEOs, CHROs, and compensation leaders should collaborate to examine pay strategies for the organization's top talent. *In practice, high-performing employees with high potential in pivotal roles should be paid far above market averages, especially when there is an acute shortage of talent in those jobs.* In addition, long-term incentives should be used in efforts to retain these employees. Nonfinancial rewards and perks should also be given in creative, highly customized ways to keep these key employees engaged in their work and committed to the organization.

HR and compensation leaders should also reevaluate the pay and reward practices for employees in nonpivotal job roles. Acceptable levels of turnover and engagement should be determined for employees in these positions, and companies should seek to pay out only a limited amount of financial capital to retain workers in these jobs. It should go without saying that low performers shouldn't receive pay increases, and in some cases should be asked to leave the organization.

Research shows that the cost of employee turnover ranges from 50 to 200 percent of an employee's annual salary based on the type and level of job he or she holds. These costs are considerable even for medium-sized companies with moderate rates of turnover.[1] Having pivotal employees defect costs even more, since their impact on an organization is greater than that of other workers and they're usually harder to replace.

While pay isn't the be-all and end-all mechanism in retaining pivotal talent, it clearly plays the starring role. Nonfinancial rewards like learning opportunities, challenging assignments, promotions, work-life balance, an ability to work remotely, and other perks are vital in themselves, but they still play a secondary role in the retention equation.

Two research studies conducted jointly by Korn Ferry, WorldatWork, and Loyola University surveyed senior corporate reward executives in more than 600 organizations.[2] The researchers found that pivotal talent leave organizations for three key reasons:

1. An opportunity to earn more pay elsewhere (77 percent)
2. Pay levels that were perceived as unfair compared with those of outside organizations (58 percent)
3. Pay levels that were perceived as unfair relative to the employee's contribution to the company (53 percent)

According to one recent salary budget survey, 95 percent or more of organizations provide a base salary increase to 95 percent or more of their employees.[3] That means, in essence, that an entire workforce gets a salary increase. Tom McMullen, a senior client partner and compensation expert at Korn Ferry, said few of the organizations in the previously referenced study provided adequate differentiation in pay increases between average and superior employees. The majority of organizations provide 1.5 times difference or less in increases between the average and superior performers. That means superiors receive 4.5 percent when average performers receive standard 3 percent increases. "Not much to capture their attention," McMullen says.

McMullen suggests that instead of giving 95 percent of employees a salary increase, organizations should consider rewarding only 65 to 75 percent of employees in a given year. Some workers wouldn't receive an increase due to their poor performance—perhaps 5 to 10 percent—and as many as 20 to 25 percent wouldn't receive any increase in any year due to already being paid fairly high compared with the market average and their peers. McMullen says getting to the ceiling of a pay range shouldn't be considered an entitlement for employees, especially in cases where employee base salaries are already 15 to 25 percent above market average. He suggests stretching out the timing of the annual increase review to 18 to 24 months for this group that's paid above market averages. The math would result in the typical 3 percent salary increase budget becoming 4 to 4.6 percent for those receiving it, *with the best performers receiving double-digit salary increases in companies with good performance distributions.*

GOOGLE

Pay Unfairly

In his book *Work Rules!*, Laszlo Bock writes that Google is one organization (and broader industry) that has successfully taken pay differentiation for top talent to an extreme. In the chapter "Pay Unfairly," Bock, the former senior vice president of people operations at Google, reports that:

> At Google, we do have situations where two people doing the same work can have a hundred times difference in their impact and in their rewards. For example, there have been situations where one person received a stock award of $10,000, and another working in the same area received $1,000,000. This isn't the norm, but the range of rewards at almost any level can easily vary by 300 to 500 percent, and even then there is plenty of room for outliers. In fact, we have many cases where people at more "junior" levels make far more than average performers at more "senior" levels. It's a natural result of having greater impact, and a compensation system that recognizes that impact.[6]

Bock goes on to describe the two capabilities needed to pull this off well:

> One is a very clear understanding of what impact is derived from the role in question (which requires a complementary awareness of how much is due to context:

Did the market move in a lucky way? How much of this was a result of a team effort or the brand of the company? Is the achievement a short- or long-term win?) . . . . If you're adopting a system like this, the only way to stay within budget is to give smaller rewards to the poorer performers, or even the average ones. That won't feel good initially, but take comfort in knowing that you've now given your best people a reason to stay with you, and everyone else a reason to aim higher.

The other capability is having managers who understand the reward system well enough that they can explain to the recipient and to others who might ask if word were to get out exactly why a reward was so high and what any employee can do to achieve a similar reward.[7]

This second point is very important. "If you can't explain to employees the basis for such a wide range of awards," Bock notes, "and can't give them specific ways to improve their own performance to these superb levels, you will breed a culture of jealousy and resentment."[8] Maintaining this type of compensation system is hard work. But it will ultimately create more work in the long run when your top talent walks out because you aren't paying them enough. Comparing Google with other organizations on pay, he suggests, "Maybe that's why most companies don't bother. It's hard work to have pay ranges where someone can make two or even ten times more than someone else. But it's much harder to watch your highest-potential and best people walk out the door. It makes you wonder which companies are really paying unfairly: the ones where the best people make far more than average, or the ones where everyone is paid the same."

Growing Pay Transparency

An organization's top performers have more access than ever before to industry pay averages and to what their peers at other organizations are compensated. Employees and potential recruits can easily find compensation-related data through online databases and social media, including sites like Salary.com, Vault.com, or Glassdoor. That pay transparency makes it harder for organizations to pay pivotal talent in ways that aren't commensurate with their significant contribution to the company. If their compensation isn't adequately differentiated from that of other employees or below what peers at other companies earn, such market intelligence will likely cause them to jump ship. Organizations that put an artificial ceiling on the earning power of pivotal talent risk losing these individuals to competitors. If HR, compensation leaders, or line managers simply turn their backs on pivotal talent after they've hit a pay ceiling, they can expect many of those top performers to exit stage left.

Pay Equity

Recent headlines abound that are related to pay discrimination lawsuits at major corporations including Google, Qualcomm, and Merck. It is clear at this point that in order to ensure fair pay practices for men and women and to create a high-performance culture and superior employee experience, more leading companies are examining pay equity.

Equal pay for equal work is a global issue. Legislation often applies to gender but may soon apply to other groups including race, age, ethnicity, and religion, although protected groups vary by country. Today mandatory reporting obligations on pay fairness exist in at least 18 countries. Many more countries have signed agreements but are not yet fully complying. Iceland, for example, is considering a bill that would require public and private businesses to prove that they offer equal pay.

To evaluate and as necessary resolve pay disparities, organizations must follow this three-step process:

1. Investigate the magnitude of the pay gaps and identify the root cause of gender or other group differences by investigating the performance and broader talent management practices. Be careful not to overestimate the size of the gap, and work to get fair comparisons. Also keep in mind global data as one guide. A Korn Ferry study looking at pay data for 8.7 million people in 33 countries that range from small to large identified that the "headline gap" in pay between men and woman is 17.6 percent, but when comparing people at the same level, the gap is reduced to 6.6 percent. Comparing people at the same level in the same company, the gap is further reduced to 2.2 percent; and finally when comparing men and women at the same level, same function, and same company, the gap is 1.6 percent.[4] Of course these gaps vary by country, as Figure 7.1 shows.

2. Once pay equity gaps for people doing comparable work are known, it is necessary to create a set of principles, practices, and a new design on pay to fix the problem. This step begins when key stakeholders establish a point of view on pay that includes thresholds for treatment of employee groups, criteria to use when paying the same or different, and explanations for how they will be more inclusive on pay. They also must determine funding mechanisms for rightsizing payment gaps. This may include paying less to employees in less pivotal roles to be cost neutral and able to fund more competitive and equal pay for employees regardless of gender who are in pivotal roles, because the stakeholders need world-class talent to execute strategy. Finally this step must include adjustments to reward and talent processes to ensure fairness across different groups of employees at point of hiring, evaluating, promoting, developing, and retaining.

3. The last step is to implement and sustain changes. This requires that governance models are established that involve legal, HR, and line manager alignment and role clarity. When there are changes to job classifications that impact levels or methods of employee compensation, these changes must be clearly communicated to all who are impacted. The last recommendation at point of implementation is that

FIGURE 7.1 Pay disparities in 10 countries

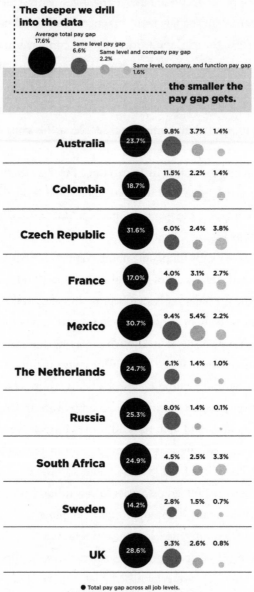

The deeper we drill into the data

Average total pay gap 17.6%

Same level pay gap 6.6%

Same level and company pay gap 2.2%

Same level, company, and function pay gap 1.6%

the smaller the pay gap gets.

Australia	23.7%	9.8%	3.7%	1.4%
Colombia	18.7%	11.5%	2.2%	1.4%
Czech Republic	31.6%	6.0%	2.4%	3.8%
France	17.0%	4.0%	3.1%	2.7%
Mexico	30.7%	9.4%	5.4%	2.2%
The Netherlands	24.7%	6.1%	1.4%	1.0%
Russia	25.3%	8.0%	1.4%	0.1%
South Africa	24.9%	4.5%	2.5%	3.3%
Sweden	14.2%	2.8%	1.5%	0.7%
UK	28.6%	9.3%	2.6%	0.8%

● Total pay gap across all job levels.
● Same level pay gap.
● Same level and company pay gap.
● Same level, company, and function pay gap.

What's more, as this graphic of 10 of the 33 countries shows, the data tell the same story around the world.

feedback loops are established back to a steering committee on the impact of pay changes on attraction, retention, and individual and organizational performance.

The Korn Ferry research is clear that when managing pay equity well, trust in leadership improves, employee engagement goes up, turnover goes down, employer brand improves, workforce diversity increases, and companywide performance gets better. Conversely organizations with lower pay equity experience increased risk of litigation, lower engagement, labor union unrest, higher attrition, and shareholder disapproval.[5]

"Practice Trumps Policy"

In the previously referenced joint Korn Ferry Hay Group, WorldatWork, and Loyola research study, respondents reported the top three strategies they most often used to retain key employees:

1. Having ongoing discussions with key talent about their future with the organization (80 percent)
2. Paying pivotal talent above the labor market (75 percent)
3. Creating a succession plan to replace individuals critical to success (74 percent) and developing employees as candidates to replace key employees who may leave (73 percent)

In interviews with survey participants, the study's authors found that *most organizations still did not have substantial differences in the overarching reward strategy for key (or pivotal) talent versus other employee groups.* This is a case where "practice trumps policy" in HR. In practice, most organizations expressed a stated intent that top talent should be earning more than others at comparable job levels. A number of organizations reported that they target the 75th percentile total cash for top talent versus the 50th to 60th percentile cash for other employees, and most said they regularly assess pay differentials between the two groups.

Yet while respondents viewed these processes as critical to retaining key talent, many also thought they were falling short when executing these areas. For example, only 69 percent thought they were "very effective or effective" at discussing with pivotal employees their future opportunities with the company; just 73 thought they were "very effective or effective" at paying pivotal employees above the labor market; and only 64 percent thought they "very effective or effective" at developing employees who may replace key employees who leave.

A primary driver of employee retention beyond pay is the opportunity for career advancement. In a separate study that examined employees who plan to stay at their organization for more than two years, a Hay Group employee opinion database found 64 percent reported "confidence in an ability to achieve career objectives with the company." Conversely, for those planning to leave the organization within two years, only 31 percent had similar confidence in their ability to achieve career objectives.

Respondents to the Korn Ferry, WorldatWork, Loyola study used two tactics when attempting to provide differentiation in compensation for pivotal talent:

1. OFF-CYCLE OR MIDYEAR BASE SALARY ADJUSTMENTS TO PROVIDE ACCELERATED INCREASES. Most organizations reported assessing this on a yearly basis as opposed to a "career income" or multiyear income basis.

2. ADDITIONAL RESTRICTED STOCK GRANTS OR CASH BONUS PAYMENTS IN LIEU OF STOCK. These are typically provided in addition to the provisions of the core short-term incentive/long-term incentive (STI/LTI) programs in place and are designed as a way to deliver additional compensation to key talent because of their disproportionate impact on the business.

Despite spending vast sums on compensation, most organizations don't measure the impact of that spending on individual or organizational performance, lacking the high-quality data necessary to make good talent decisions. Too many compensation and reward practices are still accepted at face value and not questioned at the C-suite level.

A majority of organizations in the Korn Ferry, WorldatWork, Loyola study (53 percent) said either they do not formally evaluate the effectiveness of methods for retaining and developing key talent, or they rely only on informal feedback from employees and managers. Of the remaining 47 percent who formally measure the impact of their efforts, the primary ways they do it are through review, employee opinion surveys, or examination of employee turnover data.

How Do You Differentiate Pay Without Performance Ratings?

The ongoing revolution in performance management practices has seen many organizations do away with their performance ratings. As detailed in Chapter 4, companies are abandoning their annual performance appraisals in favor of more frequent, user-friendly check-in systems and new approaches designed to make the process more focused on improving future performance than on reviewing past results.

As a part of this transformation, many companies have eliminated review ratings tied to base salary increases and incentive pay. Some are replacing the link between performance reviews and compensation by placing greater emphasis on more in-depth and frequent performance discussions and future-focused coaching and development.

The list of reasons why companies are scuttling ratings is long, according to McMullen. Included are the facts that ratings are inefficient because managers spend more time determining and defending ratings than talking to employees about their performance; that ratings lack objectivity because they are overly reliant on an individual manager's perception and aren't always accurate; and that the use of ratings hasn't ensured that managers are truly differentiating the pay and rewards that go with them.[9]

So how are companies that have eliminated ratings ensuring that they are paying for performance as well as coaching and developing employees in productive ways?

McMullen and Katie Lemaire, an organization effectiveness and performance management leader with Korn Ferry, discovered in their research and consulting work that organizations have two approaches to this dilemma. One group of companies was interested in eliminating ratings altogether without addressing the frequency or quality of performance dialogue, or their overall approach to compensation allocation. Yet without ongoing feedback, it's unlikely that employee and manager performance will improve in that scenario. Also, if there isn't more clarity on what companies really mean by pay for performance, removing ratings from the process won't change managers' behaviors, and there will likely even be a reduction in clarity about how pay for performance is defined.

The second group of companies has eliminated ratings but changed the process and timing of performance goal setting, the process and ownership of performance feedback, and the role that managers play in making compensation decisions. These organizations start change at the top, with senior leaders modeling behavior and investing in the capabilities of other leaders to create a new culture of "performance dialogue."

By eliminating ratings, there is often greater accountability for line managers in these companies in terms of base salary and STI and LTI allocation decisions because they're no longer reliant on algorithms tied to performance ratings, forced rankings, or forced distribution. *This second group of companies holds business unit managers accountable for making compensation trade-off decisions just as they're held accountable for making other financial decisions in running their units.*

Creating User-Friendly Comp and Reward Systems

To make compensation and rewards a more strategic component of talent management systems, organizations also must improve the way they communicate plans and guidelines, opting for greater transparency where possible.

Korn Ferry research has found that more than two-thirds of surveyed companies do not view their rewards communication programs to be effective, and only about one-third of organizations report that most of their employees understand their rewards philosophy.[10] The data shows that only 62 percent of companies have their rewards philosophy documented, and McMullen believes that if a philosophy is not written down, it is difficult to communicate across the organization.

Line managers are a key to improved comp and reward communications, but they need more help from HR. Employees tend to trust their immediate managers more than anyone else in the company. HR needs to help identify and leverage the best rewards communications practices, and to provide the toolkit that line managers need as questions and issues arise from the workforce.

In today's employee-engagement-obsessed environment, it's hard to believe that organizations don't involve managers or employees in the design and evaluation of rewards programs, but according to McMullen, that is still the case. His research finds only 20 percent of organizations engage their employees and only 40 percent involve their managers in these decisions.

That reality is that companies are designing and implementing programs without much input from the customers they service, McMullen says. Given that finding, it's no surprise that many organizations still don't have a good understanding of what employees truly value in rewards. Companies need to take more steps to understand individual preferences in rewards—especially where it concerns pivotal talent—and modify programs, so they include nonfinancial rewards and perks that truly motivate top performers.

Korn Ferry research also finds that employee engagement improves when employees and managers are involved in the design and launch of their compensation and reward programs.

New user-friendly technologies can also help companies manage their reward programs more strategically and efficiently. Platforms and software apps now on the market address three major questions that compensation and reward professionals want to know: (1) whether their pay structures are competitive, (2) whether their reward programs are internally equitable, and (3) if their compensation practices align with company policy. These technologies typically give users self-service access to pay databases for benchmarking purposes and mature analytics to improve their reward practices.

Even more innovative technology platforms have been integrating market data on rewards with insight into the strategic value of given employees. These systems algorithmically account for pay level variation based on user inputs related to geography, industry, function, level, required competencies, traits, experiences, likely engagement drivers, and job responsibilities. *To understand the structure of jobs in an organization, the capabilities and engagement drivers of people based on reliable and predictively powerful measures, and to align these data with pay insights is the holy grail of strategic talent management.* The integration of these data sets provide the insight needed to retain virtually any employee, but is especially important to use when trying to hold onto talent who could cripple an organization by leaving to join a competitor.

While there will always be a need to control salary growth and comply with government regulations, taking a rigid approach to compensating and rewarding pivotal talent can mean being penny-wise and pound-foolish and driving top talent out the door. By bravely and creatively differentiating pay and nonfinancial rewards for those who make a disproportionate impact on an organization, reward professionals will help ensure that their companies remain a competitive force far into the future.

Review and Action Items

1. Employee expenses represent a massive portion of any company's total costs. Strategic management of these costs is paramount to attracting, engaging, and retaining top talent as aggressive reward practices with pivotal talent will in turn deliver outsized results.

2. As important as it is to differentiate business results from (among other things) very aggressive compensation practices, it is critical to first understand the value of each role to the execution of strategy and then very accurately measure the performance of incumbents in pivotal roles. Across industries and roles this confidence is very frequently missing. Organizations must solve this puzzle before they can unlock the full potential to beat their competitors.

3. Research on the methods and frequency of the evaluation of pay programs is reviewed, data across 33 countries on the recent movement to drive pay equity is summarized, and new ideas for how to communicate and differentiate pay practices are shared.

CHAPTER 8

TALENT ACQUISITION

There are many sayings that recruiters and hiring managers use to justify hiring talent from the outside. One is "You can't train IQ." Another comes from professional sports: "You can't coach height, speed, or strength." And one of my favorites is "An ounce of selection is worth a pound of development." These declarations make replacing poor performers seem easy and give the impression that external hires are the panacea to solving all performance problems.

In reality, it is not that simple. Even at the CEO level, when presumed success in a role would be relatively high, a *Harvard Business Review* article notes, "The Center for Creative Leadership estimates that two out of every five (or 40 percent) of CEOs fail within 18 months."[1] Turnover in the retail industry is far worse. One study reports that the median turnover rate is 67 percent for part-time retail employees.[2]

And turnover is expensive. Even the best people leaders use the line "That guy was a bad hire" to excuse the costs incurred and havoc wreaked when selection decisions go sour. One study found that it costs, on average, $3,328 (or 16 percent of one year's salary) to find, hire, and train a replacement for one minimum-wage employee. Of course, the actual costs are much higher, including lost funds for hiring, onboarding, and training, the cost of errors and lower productivity during the training period, and the impact on the company culture and other employees' productivity.[3] These mistakes are very costly, and organizations can ill afford to tolerate the failure modes associated with "old-school" talent acquisition practices, which seem to put the wrong people in the wrong place at the wrong time.

The best way to manage the high costs and risks associated with talent acquisition is to redesign processes so that they follow the three principles of this book.

Strategic Talent Acquisition

Terminating poor performers with little analysis of why they failed and whether their troubles could have been predicted pre-hire and then quickly refilling the same position with the same process may meet the definition of insanity. Prior to hiring, it's important to establish an organizational talent road map that provides the direction needed to ensure that talent acquisition spend is filling in skill sets that increase the competitiveness of a function, business unit, and organization overall. A strategically derived talent forecast is not hard to translate into a hiring road map, but this aligned thinking is often overlooked. One study reported that 61 percent of talent acquisition professionals say their recruitment team is not aligned to their organization's business objectives. Worse, 29 percent admit they don't have a strategic workforce plan at all.[4] Results from the same survey revealed that only 39 percent of respondents report that their recruitment team is aligned to their organization's business objectives for the next one to three years.[5]

When the foresight exists to hire strategically, the results can be awe inspiring. Sometimes the strategy calls for change or transformation that only an outside leader can bring. Famous examples of boards or owners making the tough call to change current leadership and existing strategy include:

- **STEVE JOBS'S RETURN TO APPLE.** Prior to his hire, the company had a market capitalization of $3 billion. When Jobs came in, he was given the opportunity to build his own team and to design and execute a completely new business strategy. Eventually, Apple became the world's most valuable company, and in 2018 it became the first ever company to reach a market cap of more than $1 trillion.

- FORD MOTOR COMPANY'S CALCULATED RISK HIRING ALAN MULALLY FROM BOEING. Mulally led the troubled automaker from a $12.7 billion loss and near bankruptcy in 2006 to earning $7.2 billion in 2013, the year before he retired (more details about Mulally's assessed capabilities are given in Chapter 11).
- BOSTON RED SOX HIRING THEO EPSTEIN AS GENERAL MANAGER. In 2002 Epstein became the youngest general manager in the history of Major League Baseball. He helped turn around the Boston Red Sox, and in 2004 the team won its first World Series championship in 86 years. In case you think that was a fluke, the Red Sox operating as "the team Theo built" won additional series titles in 2007, 2013, and 2018. Good leadership or dumb luck? In 2011 Epstein resigned from the Red Sox and became the president of baseball operations for the Chicago Cubs, which in 2016 won its first World Series in 108 years.

When adding the people necessary to drive an organization's success, talent acquisition intersects with strategy. Consider Japanese pharmaceutical company Otsuka. The company wanted to increase revenue by introducing new products into North America. It built a new salesforce and hired 500 sales executives within six months, while concurrently developing executive leadership to support growth.[6]

Sourcing and attracting large quantities of strong talent cannot happen unless the organization really understands its own reputation as an employer. Lots of this information can be found online via social media platforms, and employers must stand ready to defend (or better, to proactively overcome) any concerns that might drive talent away. The employee value proposition (EVP) must persuasively communicate the advantages, and these messages must be compellingly presented on career websites, in social media, and in all recruitment collateral.

Once the recruiting function is aligned with the business on the talent forecasts and the EVP has been clearly outlined, innovative sourcing strategies must be established. The next step is to answer key questions about how to tap into talent communities, leverage social media, build a reputation on campus, establish employee referral programs, and select recruiting firms and agencies. All these sources of talent should have expected levels of return. Each source of talent should be evaluated based on the quality *and* quantity of people delivered to the business. Performance levels by source of talent will later dictate the amount of resources allocated in subsequent years.

Mind the Gap—Talent Acquisition Analytics

Not just a safety reminder when boarding the Tube in the London Underground, "minding the gap" is also an important metric in talent acquisition analytics. Minding the data gap, found at the intersection of talent and strategy, has several dimensions. The aforementioned EVP, sourcing, and talent forecasting categories all have quantifiable information that make or break the ability to attract strong talent. Data related to time, cost, and quality of hires is also essential to business success. It's a big problem when large gaps exist between the EVP needed to attract top talent away from competitors and an organization's current EVP levels. "Good" and sometimes even "poor" businesses can limp along for a while, but until they have a distinctive strategy, results will suffer. To design and execute said strategy requires the ability to attract and retain the best, and this won't happen unless candidates and incumbents like their role, pay, colleagues, environment, and the organization overall. If a quick Internet search reveals that employees are not passionate about the product or service they are producing, then forget it—candidates won't join.

When the wrong candidate is selected quickly and inexpensively, the cost per hire and time to fill a role are low, but time and money are not actually saved. Benchmarks for the efficiency metrics really vary by industry, level, role, and a variety of other factors, and generally lower numbers are better—except when it comes to quality of hire. It is prudent to baseline current efficiency metrics, benchmark these levels, and then try to improve over time. If pivotal talent is to be hired, however, cost per hire and time to fill metrics must be subordinated to quality of hire, and this data must be cross-validated for accuracy.

To maximize quality of hire, it's very hard to outperform what decades of science have taught us. The meta-analytics on the power of single predictors is conclusive. General mental abilities or the ability to make strong decisions and to learn new tasks is the strongest single predictor of job performance across all jobs. Second strongest is a well-structured measure of integrity. High scorers on integrity tests are those people who show up for work, follow rules, and act in the best interest of their employer.

When the volume of applicants is high, the statistical power of online measures of these traits help screen candidates accurately and can be delivered at low cost. When hiring in the United States, be cautious about avoiding risks associated with measures of cognitive ability, as it will often have adverse impact on protected classes.

The most practical way to hire while involving hiring managers is to design selection solutions around the unique job requirements; choose a combination of instruments to balance accuracy, time, cost, and insight for the candidate and hiring team. Some consider this a "mixed model," which posits that an assessment must be designed based on the interaction between the job requirements and measures of the candidates. This approach optimizes predictive power and the face validity of the experience. Results with this approach are impressive. When comparing strong and weak performers on a readiness assessment using multiple methods, Maynard Goff reports that "a person in the top quartile of assessment scores is 8 times more likely to be a top quartile performer than a person with an assessment score in the bottom quartile."[7]

When the risks of a bad hire are high and if mistakes are costly, a solution should factor in personality traits (including facets of a derailing personality), cognitive ability, experiences, and drivers of motivation. Conducting structured interviews and simulations, or asking for work samples are additional methods that offer strong predictive power and allow candidates to demonstrate their ability to handle job challenges very similar to the open role. When administered by experienced assessors who understand the power of the analytics, each component will explain unique variance in the future job performance of the candidates.

As explained in the Johnson & Johnson case study in Chapter 12, using a best-in-class selection system will compare internal and external candidates on measures statistically proven to differentiate job performance. Often such solutions will allow comparisons of candidates not only with one another but with external benchmarks. These comparisons quantify and qualify what "great" looks like. When risking the placement of a near stranger into a role that could have a multibillion-dollar impact on an organization, it is helpful to know, for example, that the person is in the 98th percentile of strategic thinking and in the 91st percentile of results agility, but is in the 4th percentile of self-awareness and has several derailment risks. Overall this candidate may be in the midrange but is far weaker than another who may be almost as strong on strategy and results agility but far stronger at leading teams.

The stories of bad hires and arrogant hiring managers who insisted their "gut" was correct are endless, but the data doesn't lie. Designing reliable, valid, legally defensible methods for filling roles is no longer time consuming or expensive. Assessments designed from job profiles powerfully manage the risk and expense of bad hire. Although not perfect, they repeatedly lend insight that cannot be gained any other way.

For more data, case studies, and testimony on the power of assessment analytics, see Chapters 2 (analytics), 6 (succession planning), and 1 (boards and CEO succession).

Candidate Expectations and Experiences

It's simple really. Active and passive candidates alike want to learn about opportunities that are a direct match with their interests, and they hate wasting time talking with recruiters (real people or chatbots) whose processes complicate their lives. Candidates expect the recruiting process to be quick, convenient, accurate, engaging, comprehensive, . . . and fun.

But it is not. Time is often wasted, questions go unanswered, hard feelings are created, uncertainty exists, black holes seem to swallow information, and too seldom perfect matches between candidate and employer are made. Worse, many candidates never find their perfect job due to the inefficiencies in the labor market matching process. As a result too many valuable people are left underemployed, undercompensated, and disengaged.

To fix this process employers who are serious about finding and hiring the best must analyze every touch point they have with active and passive candidates. They must spot failure modes where otherwise strong candidates receive mixed messages, get frustrated, and drop out. They need to examine how each touch point compares with those of the companies with which they compete for talent, and then they must look outside their industry for solutions that address each failure.

Often low-cost solutions, which address major concerns and candidate quality, can be found. Inexpensive solutions may include:

- **COMMUNICATE THE PROCESS.** Clearly communicating what a candidate may expect in the process prevents candidates from getting impatient and looking elsewhere when they don't hear from you. Even if the process is long, managing expectations can defuse frustration.
- **DESCRIBE THE WORK.** Giving a complete and honest explanation of the job responsibilities, culture, and challenges allows candidates to opt in or out.
- **RESPECT THE CANDIDATE.** Limit the number of steps and interviews, give and receive feedback throughout the process, and trust will be built.

More extensive efforts may need to be made when the EVP doesn't line up with the corporate brand, or if the opportunities consist of hard-to-change concerns like geographically undesirable work locations, poor working conditions, or ethical concerns related to employee-employer relations.

If the selection ratio, or number of applicants to openings, is high, elaborate assessment methods may be used, and it's a hiring manager's market. But during periods of low unemployment, the war for talent is fought every day. Ultimately, a candidate must select the employer. If there is a strong fit with the work, the hiring manager, the team, the culture, and the organizational mission, candidates will enthusiastically sign up. Top talent will want to join an organization that pays well and creates engaging touch points related to each step in the hiring process.

Hiring-Team Challenges and Opportunities

Recruiters like to clear open requisitions from their desks as fast and inexpensively as possible, but they learned years ago that hired talent must be great and must be retained. Simply trying to close jobs with any warm body is no longer tolerable.

To do the job well, recruiters must help themselves; yet a survey in 2017 showed that less than 50 percent of talent acquisition leaders are taking advantage of recruitment technologies such as applicant tracking systems, video interviewing, or online assessment tools.[8]

In an effort to get better and faster, many recruiters are warming up to the idea of getting help from technology. The above survey found that 64 percent of respondents said AI and big data have changed how their organizations recruit. Most interestingly, 87 percent said they are "excited" by the prospect of working more closely with AI, and only 11 percent thought AI would replace their jobs.

So what can be done today? Korn Ferry's professional recruitment business is now using AI in the following ways to deliver extraordinary results:[9]

Utilizing a database of about 250 million individual work profiles across the globe—which is augmented by human input from Korn Ferry professionals—we precisely match job descriptions with candidates and identify high performers in specific job categories.

We've imported a Bayesian network, or a probabilistic model, into our database to find patterns and relationships, and trace individual histories to better understand what a successful person looks like in a particular position. For example, in a search for a global automotive maker, we discovered that in one country there was a significant movement of executives from the luxury goods sector to the automotive sector—a relationship that wasn't obvious otherwise. After discovering this successful hiring trend, our client applied that insight to recruiting in several other countries and quality of hires improved dramatically.

For mid- and lower-level professional hires, we use chatbots to help candidates research job openings and to schedule interviews, reducing administrative work and provide a candidates with a quick way to determine if there is a viable opportunity in an organization. Using a natural language processing technology, a chatbot can engage a person in a conversation, through either textual or auditory means.

In addition to sourcing talent, AI can also be used to analyze the value of time spent on each hire, thereby improving the user experience for both candidates and hiring teams. One study looked at average number of interviews per hire across roles from countries all over the world. The study found an average of 13 interviews per job filled.[10]

Realizing it was often very close to that number of interviews on average, Google did the math on the efficacy of spending so much time (and money). Laszlo Bock writes in *Work Rules!* that when Google analyses revealed that four interviews was enough to predict whether or not a candidate should be hired with 86 percent confidence and that each additional interview only added another 1 percent of confidence, hiring managers implemented a "rule of four" that limits the number of times interview candidates come on-site to four. This change shaved Google's hiring time down to an average of 47 days compared with 90 to 180 days.[11] Consistent with this book's recommendations to use multiple methods to assess talent, Google adds predictive power by adding measures of cognitive ability, leadership, role-related knowledge using work samples, and fit for company and role, known as a candidate's "Googleyness."

Limiting the number of interviews and focusing assessments only on predictors of success on the job will save time. New methods of assessment also enable the collection of more accurate assessment data faster than ever before. These methods include computer-adaptive and forced-choice item response methodologies. Using gaming in assessment is also clearly on the rise, but it can be expensive to develop. Other cautions related to gaming are reliability, validity, job relatedness, and therefore (at least in the United States) legal defensibility. Fun experiences clearly do engage candidates, but they cannot come at the expense of high-quality selection decisions.

A COSTLY OVERSIGHT

Poor Onboarding for New Leaders Has Bottom-Line Fallout

Many organizations fail to provide the proper support when people are promoted or transition into new or different leadership roles with increased and evolved responsibilities. The result is that new leaders often take much longer than necessary to get up to speed or to operate at optimal levels in new roles.

"Even the most skilled executive faces pressure to add value quickly in their new role," says Dee Gaeddert, a senior partner at Korn Ferry. "A good onboarding process will ensure that a new executive understands the 'lay of the land,' all of the nuances that make the difference between gaining traction quickly while navigating seamlessly versus struggling to have impact, or worse, derailing."

The failure to properly onboard a new hire in a leadership position can have major financial implications—for both individuals and organizations. The average organization-wide cost of onboarding per year, according to Korn Ferry survey respondents, is $8.3 million, ranging up to $200 million.

Although this sum seems sizable at first glance, the estimate may not capture the full picture. Korn Ferry has found that 40 percent of executives in new roles fail within the first 18 months, and some estimates say this costs organizations as much as $2.7 million per executive. If organizations rely on fresh leadership for critical market initiatives and they fail to provide the proper support so those leaders can thrive, companies can put their future at risk.

While it takes about six months for a new staffer to reach a breakeven point where the person's contribution equals the cost of hiring, it is widely accepted that it takes a full year for leaders to perform at full speed in new roles. *Yet more than half of respondents to the Korn Ferry study said their organizations expect optimal performance in six months or less,* largely because there's a faster pace in business today and greater expectations to produce results. The fact that research based reality and executive expectations for a new leader performing at full speed are misaligned presents another opportunity for HR to close the gap and help the business.

Recruiting Process Outsourcing

Increasingly organizations are realizing that operating at the intersection of strategy and talent acquisition is so challenging and fast moving, that they choose to focus on business strategy and partner with others by outsourcing all or part of the recruiting process. The RPO (recruiting process outsourcing) choice often comes down to whether organizations have the capabilities and resources necessary to deliver the quantity and quality of candidates needed to run their business at the right times and places. Some organizations manage the many stages of talent acquisition well through hiring peaks and troughs, using internally staffed HR teams. Others choose to partner externally to redesign their EVP, manage integrated sourcing campaigns, and onboard talent.

RPO CASE STUDY

Alcon, a Division of Novartis

With $6 billion in 2017 revenue, Alcon has always been true to its commitment to developing innovative eye care products and technologies.[12] In 2010 Alcon joined the Novartis global family of companies to become the world leader in eye care.

Alcon understood early on that to achieve its goal in eye care, it would need to attract the best and brightest talent in the industry. The company also recognized the many facets and intricacies of talent acquisition. "In our case the decision was made to go with an outsourced provider because our talent acquisition function was not able to adequately serve the business. Consequently we were overspending on talent acquisition services by using a myriad of agencies all across the world," says Alcon vice president and global head of talent management and organizational development Jeff Bettinger. The company wanted to leverage the scalability, sourcing expertise, and recruitment technology of an RPO provider to support its growth in a cost-effective way. As Alcon continued to invest in outsourced recruitment, the potential of an RPO to provide more than just cost savings became apparent. Jeff and the rest of the leadership team saw an opportunity to improve their employer brand and the experiences of their customers, candidates, and hiring managers.

The scope of the original engagement included the end-to-end recruitment of 850 hires a year for five years in roles across research and development, manufacturing, quality, sales, and corporate functions. This dedicated delivery team, led by a project director, worked on-site at Alcon headquarters in Fort Worth. The team includes a social media, diversity, and inclusion manager; a compliance manager; and a data and analytics manager—roles that are not typically found on an RPO team. It was Jeff's decision to include these roles. At the time, he was Alcon's global head of talent acquisition, and he recognized the value of leveraging social platforms and diversity recruitment to reach candidates and the important role that data analytics could play in connecting recruitment initiatives to the top line.

Within the first six months of the engagement, Alcon had met its cost-saving goals and other strategic milestones. Three years earlier, Alcon's agency usage ranged between 60 and 80 percent; now it is below 5 percent. When Korn Ferry's Professional Recruiting team came in, it identified an eight-day savings in the company's recruitment process.

"When you multiply that by several hundred [sales] reps over the course of a year in hiring, you're talking about a seven figure addition you can make to the top line because of process improvements," Jeff notes. He was quick to add that didn't even take into account the differences in time to fill and quality of hire that Korn Ferry has realized over the course of the engagement.

The on-site team has increased the number of diverse candidate slates by 100 percent and enabled Alcon's HR business partners to make better decisions with metrics tracked through Korn Ferry's Foresight tool. Hiring manager satisfaction jumped to 89 percent from 40 percent, where it stood before Korn Ferry came in. That score has been holding strong, and Jeff admits, "I just can't tell you how dramatically different that feels to a leadership team."

Conclusion

The world of talent acquisition has changed dramatically in just the last few years. With all the new technologies, AI tools, web-scraping capabilities, social media, and many databases on talent, this pace of change will never slow down. It's hard to imagine that just a few years ago we were responding to help-wanted sections of local newspapers by mailing résumés and then crossing our fingers to get a phone call from a recruiter.

Today hiring teams use collaborative tools to quickly and accurately gain alignment on a success profile, submit that profile, and watch as slates of quality talent populate recruiters' desktop apps instantaneously. In seconds recruiters not only know the scarcity/abundance of talent and exactly where to find qualified people, they also know who these candidates really are based on extremely accurate assessments. They also know how each candidate's pay compares with the market for a given role in the geography where they're hiring. They can see a list of skills that may be difficult to develop in each candidate, and if they want to see more candidates, they make supply and demand queries of talent to see which of their competitors recently hired candidates with the experiences they are seeking. These tools make it much easier to operate (or partner) in support of business strategy, with data-driven methods, to quickly talent acquisition and deliver big value to a business.

Review and Action Items

1. Too often talent acquisition professionals operate transactionally and independent of strategically derived workforce plans and build-buy targets. In doing so the opportunity to upgrade capabilities in critical areas is lost.

2. Efficiency metrics including "cost per hire" and "time to fill" have improved with the advent of new technologies, but quality-of-hire data is still lagging. Complementing interviews with statistically superior assessment methods will deliver better results.

3. Talent acquisition trends on the rise include the use of artificial intelligence for sourcing and screening, web-scraping to understand labor
   supply and demand, and recruitment process outsourcing to improve
   the cost, speed, and quality when hiring. Understanding the pros and
   cons of these methods and their impact on strategy, analytics, and the
   candidate experience is a must.

CHAPTER 9

EMPLOYEE ENGAGEMENT

Considered the greatest prize in human resources, employee engagement is often the one ingredient that CHROs believe can lead to the riches of improved employee productivity, better retention of top talent, and a stronger bottom line, if achieved. Yet while engagement does add unmistakable value to an organization, it also ranks among the most misunderstood and poorly executed areas of talent management.

It's no secret what happens when people are highly engaged, a state that the Gallup organization defines as "working with passion and finding a profound connection to one's company." Employees in such a state often produce better work, are more likely to go above and beyond to meet business goals or satisfy customers, and tend to stay with an organization longer.

But the disturbing reality of engagement is that many HR leaders spend too much time and money trying to get the wrong employees passionately connected to the company, and when they do target the right workers, their efforts often leave much to be desired. Engagement strategies should be highly tilted in favor of high-performing, high-potential employees in pivotal job roles, those workers who—if they become disengaged or, worse, leave the organization—can do tremendous financial or psychic damage to companies.

Before the war for talent began, when unemployment rates were high, management was less concerned about how engaged employees were, even their best workers. But as labor markets began to tighten and top talent grew scarce, improvements have been made, and some organizations have documented their impact.

How One Company Ties Engagement to Financial Results

Rentokil Initial is a service organization whose business results depend heavily on how engaged its employees feel, in part because of a large remote workforce. The company, with headquarters in the United Kingdom, is among the world's largest commercial pest control service providers.

Hoping to extract more value from its annual employee survey, Rentokil asked Korn Ferry to help find links between those survey outcomes and business results.

A combination of correlation and gap analysis, based on 15 months of data, revealed a direct link between "enablement"—*feeling able to get the job done*—employee retention, and gross profit margin. The study also showed the importance of engagement in health and safety outcomes and in the retention of pivotal employees in sales and service roles.

Rentokil's employee survey had traditionally provided a measure of employee engagement and helped to pinpoint areas for improvement, generating up to 2,220 local action plans from the branch to divisional levels. But moving forward, the company wanted to find clear connections between survey responses and business performance.

To find those connections, Korn Ferry undertook linkage research that looked for relationships between the employee survey data and three sets of Rentokil's key performance indicators (KPIs):

- Financial (including gross margin and revenue growth)
- Employee data (specifically retention statistics for sales and customer service people)
- Customer data around service quality and client retention

Ties to Bottom-Line Performance

Korn Ferry linked the survey data to 15 months of KPIs, using a two-phase approach to analyze the data. The first phase used statistical analysis to find correlations between survey responses and KPIs, finding many strong correlations above the range typical for these studies. Evidence from these correlations indicated a minimum six-month lag in the causal relationship between survey results and KPIs.

Then researchers used a gap analysis, looking at survey results from the top- and bottom-performing business units to pinpoint the biggest opinion gaps. Together these analyses gave Rentokil Initial the means to quantify the financial impact of changes in the survey scores.

Rentokil found it could get the biggest return on investment by making improvements in a few key areas. Creating the conditions that enable employees to do their jobs well was clearly linked to retention, gross margins, and health and safety. *The analysis showed that the Rentokil teams with the top-quartile gross margin have higher levels of enablement (more than 8 percent) than the bottom-quartile teams.*

While employee engagement is crucial, it can fade over time and lead to a frustrated workforce if people feel unable to translate their enthusiasm into action. So *enablement* is a stronger predictor of performance. At Rentokil, enablement accounted for 8 percent of variance in gross margin results. For every percentage point more that employees feel enabled, gross margin will rise by 0.5 percent. Enablement in the company was also closely linked to employee retention, particularly for service employees, where a 1 percent improvement in enablement improved retention by 0.45 percent. With the cost of replacing an employee estimated at 1.5 to 2x their annual

(continued on next page)

salary—plus opportunity costs—there was a quantifiable impact in this area.

The study also showed that engagement plays a crucial role in the retention of sales employees, a pivotal talent pool in the organization. A 1 percent improvement in engagement resulted in an improvement in retention of sales personnel of 0.39, the study found.

Finally, the study also found impacts on employee health and safety, which if poor, can result in increases in indirect costs through lost time and higher insurance rates. The study revealed that business units with good safety records were significantly more engaged (+4) and enabled (+7) than those with poorer safety records.

The Engagement Landscape

The news about employee engagement overall continues to be grim. According to Gallup's latest "State of the Global Workplace" report, 85 percent of U.S. employees are either "not engaged" or "actively disengaged" at work, contributing to an estimated $7 trillion in lost productivity.

The 67 percent of employees identified as not engaged make up most of the workforce; they aren't the worst performers, according to the Gallup study, but rather are indifferent to the organization. "They give you their time, but not their best effort or ideas," wrote Jim Harter, PhD and chief scientist of the workplace management practice at Gallup, in an article connected to the research. "They likely come to work wanting to make a difference—but nobody has ever asked them to use their strengths to make the organization better."

There's little dispute that concerted efforts to improve engagement, including the regular use of well-designed engagement surveys, can pay dividends. When compared with business units in the bottom quartile of the Gallup company's research database, those in the top quartile of engagement realize 10 percent higher customer metrics, 17 percent higher productivity, 20 percent higher sales, and 21 percent higher profitability. Organizations at the top achieve earnings-per-share growth that is more than four times that of their competitors, according to Gallup's data.

The trouble with engagement lies in how companies attempt to identify factors that create low engagement or fully disengaged workers—and the steps they take to address those problems once they're discovered.

Organizations continue to collect a significant volume of data about engagement through annual surveys, quarterly or monthly "pulse" surveys, and their internal communication platforms. These methods all gather valuable feedback on how employees feel about their jobs, their managers, their culture, and the workplace in general.

Touching base this frequently with employees follows a belief that surveying them just once a year is tantamount to reviewing financial performance or soliciting customer feedback only annually. Much can change in employee sentiment in short periods, trends that left unaddressed can lead to diminished productivity or high turnover rates. To avoid burying employees in these more frequent surveys, smart companies often divide their populations into random groups and survey a different group each month.

Although this trend toward gathering more feedback is encouraging, many of these survey approaches have one troubling practice in common—an overreliance on anonymous, aggregated responses.

Engaging Pivotal Talent

Relying only on anonymous survey feedback or using one-size-fits-all approaches to engage pivotal employees is among the biggest problems in talent management today. Given what's at stake, how companies go about engaging their most valuable employees requires a wholesale rethinking and some new approaches.

Evaluating aggregated survey results rather than pinpointing individual concerns contributes to one-size-fits-all responses to boosting engagement. This common practice works at cross-purposes with the fact that employees—and most important to this discussion, *pivotal* employees—are often motivated by vastly different drivers.

There's also a growing problem of management failing to follow up on major themes identified by employees in engagement surveys. When the walk doesn't match the talk, it can lead to discontent and low participation from workers on future surveys, as they see little evidence of how their feedback is used to create meaningful change in the workplace.

Dangers of Anonymity

A preponderance of research shows that employees are engaged by many different factors. Depending on career stage, generation, job role, gender, and other variables, people might be motivated by pay and benefits, challenging stretch assignments, learning opportunities, a sabbatical, a chance to leave a legacy, or the opportunity to mentor others in the organization. For example, job tenure is often overlooked in engagement strategies. Two employees in an organization might be the same age, but one might have 15 years of experience at the company and another could be a new hire. The experienced worker might become more engaged by a chance to leave a legacy or work on projects that build the organization's future, while the new employee could be more motivated by a chance to learn new skills or gain additional knowledge.

When aggregating data, we lose individual variance that makes the very process of engaging top talent possible. And relying only on anonymous, aggregated feedback doesn't address these highly personal engagement drivers. There's a longstanding belief in HR and other fields that if surveys aren't anonymous, employees won't be honest and data will be compromised. But some emerging research suggests otherwise. For example, one study that compared anonymous versus nonanonymous, or "named," comments by college students about the quality of their professors and university found that students in the nonanonymous group included far more detail in their written comments, suggesting feedback might be of even higher quality when anonymity is removed.[1]

As one former HR leader and current consultant said in an industry publication, "If employees prefer anonymity because they are afraid of backlash, you've got a leadership problem, not an engagement survey problem."[2]

The way that some engagement surveys are administered in companies can also prevent HR leaders from truly understanding engagement levels and from improving engagement when surveys determine it to be low. Research shows that top-performing employees tend to be the busiest and often don't fill out the surveys, meaning much of the engagement data comes from average or low-performing employees.[3] That means organizations could be getting little feedback from high-performing, high-potential employees in pivotal roles—where there's often the biggest return on investment from efforts to boost engagement.

The Missing Link in Engagement: High-Touch Leader Involvement

These prevailing misconceptions and questionable strategies impact efforts to enhance employee engagement levels. HR practitioners or other organizational leaders interpreting survey results should have a good grasp of these issues, so they can better gauge how "emotionally connected" to the company people feel, and work to make that bond stronger.

One of those misconceptions is what defines an "engaged" employee. Edward Lawler, a professor at the University of Southern California's Marshall School of Business, wrote a blog post titled "An Idiot's Guide to Employee Engagement" where he identified some primary fallacies of engagement.

One of those fallacies is a belief that "a happy worker is a productive worker." Research over several decades shows low or no correlation between job satisfaction and performance, Lawler writes. "In some cases," he notes, "there was low correlation only because performing well made employees more satisfied—not because employees worked harder *because* they were satisfied."

Satisfaction leads to *membership*, Lawler says, not *performance*. "Satisfied employees are likely to stay with a company, but not be the most productive workers," he writes.

Another fallacy is that money is not a strong driver of engagement and is only a "hygiene" factor, meaning that once employees achieve a certain level of pay, it ceases to be a motivator. "The simple fact of the matter is that for many people, it *does* motivate performance," Lawler writes. "Study after study has shown that when significant amounts of money are clearly tied to specific behaviors, those behaviors are more likely to occur."

Lawler and other organizational behavior experts believe the missing piece is *highly personalized* efforts to determine what engages different employees. Those drivers can vary significantly among individuals. "Often the best way to find out what people value is to *ask them*," Lawler states. "Usually, they are pretty good reporters of what they value. However, sometimes they don't have a high level of self-awareness, or they may feel that it is necessary to give a politically correct response." In that case it's better to observe the choices people make when choosing rewards, whether that is receiving a raise, a promotion, time off, learning opportunities, or other rewards.

Like many things in life, we make engagement too complex when in reality it is starkly simple. While there is obvious value in using surveys to measure engagement at scale, the simple act of leaders taking time to talk more frequently to their pivotal talent about the particular—and sometimes idiosyncratic—factors that keep them motivated is key to fixing the engagement problem.

Determine what their passion is, connect it to their daily work, and you'll be on the path to unleasing the power of full engagement. It may sound simple, but precious few organizations mandate that their leaders communicate in this fashion with employees on a regular basis.

To get started, select a half-dozen leaders in your organization and try the exercise that I used with a client who asked me to develop coaching skills in the company's leaders. I told this client that engaging the leaders was simple, but it starts with understanding what drives each of their direct reports. I passed out a napkin and asked them to write out the primary and secondary drivers of engagement for each of their direct reports. Unfortunately, they either had no idea or they admitted they were wrong with most of their assumptions, as leaders often assume others are driven by the same things they are. Upon asking their directs what really was important, they were instantly better able to connect with them on how to align "pay" or deliver what mattered to each individual. Engagement need not be any more complex than this simple dialogue and a little follow-up to ensure you have it right.

In short, engagement surveys should not be seen as a substitute for regular, face-to-face communication between managers and employees about engagement or performance factors. Organizations need to supplement their survey data with these high-touch efforts to discern what drives their top employees. Research shows that leaders in high-performing companies spend more one-on-one time with their pivotal talent to identify their engagement drivers—whether it's money, work challenges, more autonomy, affiliation, work-life balance, or other motivators—than low-performing companies do, and then those leaders pull out the stops to try to meet those needs.

Three Case Studies: Pivotal Talent Is Engaged by Different Drivers

One utility organization, for example, asked me to coach one of its highest-potential engineers whom the company didn't want to lose to the competition. This engineer happened to love surfing, so he was given permission to leave work and hit the waves whenever his beach webcam revealed that the surf was high. The only condition was that he maintained his high level of contribution. *Such organizations profit from the belief that elite employees have earned trust and the right to be rewarded in even the most idiosyncratic ways and should be supported in doing what they love most.*

A second coaching case of mine was a defense company whose top operations leader had very high potential and needed to be retained. He was happy to deliver very creative solutions to the company's most vexing operational challenges, on one condition: he wanted to take long weekends in the fall to attend each football game played at his alma mater, Louisiana State University. The company was happy to accommodate his travel schedule every autumn weekend, knowing it was a small price to pay to have one of its strongest leaders fully engaged.

A third coaching client of mine was in a high-potential program and was tapped to become a direct report to the CEO at one of the largest technology companies in the world. But rising to that level was not in his career plan. He told me, "I'm glad I am doing well, but to be clear, the very last thing I would ever want is to report to a member of this company's executive team!" In fact, he said if he were promoted, he'd quit. For this high-potential leader, there was no possible way to balance his family life and an executive-level job at the same time. He very clearly chose his family. The company honored his choice and went on to fill its executive vacancy from the outside.

Senior leaders need improved data and insights about the engagement drivers of pivotal talent so they can better understand the relationship between employee capabilities, potential, and engagement. The pinnacle of talent management is achieved when generating reliable, real-time data about current capabilities and future potential as well as creating accurately measured data on employee engagement. The confluence and interaction of these data sources lead to more effective talent management and more powerful engagement initiatives.

Think Your Workforce Is Highly Engaged?
Try a Pay-to-Quit Offer

Some organizations brave enough to assess the true engagement level of their workforce go beyond using surveys to deploy the ultimate litmus test of engagement: making a pay-to-quit offer.

Zappos, the online shoe retailer, was among the first to make such a bet by offering workers $4,000 to leave the company on the 90-day anniversary of their hiring. The idea behind the offer was to separate employees truly committed to working for Zappos from others who could take or leave employment or weren't thrilled with their jobs.

Amazon, which later purchased Zappos, adopted a version of this pay-to-quit offer in its fulfillment centers. Rather than receiving the offer just once during a probationary period, employees get the offer once a year, for a number of years. The first year the offer starts at $2,000 and increases by $1,000 each year until it hits a ceiling of $5,000.[4] Only a small number of Amazon employees have accepted the offer since it was first introduced.

When Zappos initially began this initiative, the belief in the human resources community was that other organizations would soon follow suit. But that hasn't been the case. Why? One human resources leader suggested it's because top executives are worried that too many of the good employees would take the money and run.[5] This talent leader wrote in a blog that "it might be the single greatest HR initiative in history that barely any organization is using."[6]

Ultimately the problem falls back to HR leaders, this expert wrote. If they believe in the power of their culture and engagement strategies, they should be willing to sell the idea of such

(continued on next page)

pay-to-quit offers to the C-suite—betting that most top employees would not take them up on the offer. "High performance cultures can afford to pay people to quit," he wrote.

Here is how Amazon CEO Jeff Bezos explained the strategy to shareholders in a memo: "The goal is to encourage folks to take a moment to think about what they really want. In the long run, an employee staying somewhere they don't want to be isn't healthy for the employee or for the company."

Summary of Steps for Strategic Engagement of Top Talent

Principle number one in this book is to establish inextricable links between people processes and strategy execution. Such links are established in engagement when leaders prioritize the most critical roles that differentiate their business from the competition. These honest and tough decisions must be made, as the resources to invest in engagement are limited and an even distribution of resources across all talent dilutes impact. Principle number two could be summarized with the expression "In God we trust . . . everyone else bring data." The data needed for strategic talent management is valid numbers on performance, potential, engagement drivers, and compensation. The third principle of this book is allowing leaders to operate quickly and simply at the intersection of strategy and data so they can invest differentially in the engagement of their top talent.

These principles can only be executed when leaders can answer the following five questions with confidence. Take a moment to answer these questions for yourself:

1. Which of the positions that report to me have the biggest impact on the execution of what I am expected to deliver?
2. Among the incumbents in my most pivotal position(s), who are the highest performers?

3. Among the highest-performing incumbents, which ones have the most potential to deliver results in bigger roles? (If this is too short a list, go build or buy more talent in the role!)

4. For each of the high-performing, high-potential incumbents in the most pivotal roles, what are their primary and secondary drivers of engagement?

5. What is my plan and timeline for helping my most valuable people get what they need so they remain highly engaged?

Of course, great leaders will be able to answer all five of these questions quickly. But in organizations where managers cannot, HR must step in.

The most courageous and ambitious organizations may seek to scale the collection of the data listed above. If they already have good data on capabilities and compensation, the next step to gather enterprise engagement data, by person, is to communicate that employee survey responses are *not* anonymous.

Despite the research cited above, some will claim that survey respondents will only offer socially desirable responses. But they do so at their peril, as this would make it harder to address their engagement drivers. If the organization is truly committed to addressing employee concerns and is courageous enough to invest differentially in engagement, then the cultural value of transparency via attributable survey responses would pay many dividends.

Integrating data sets on performance, potential, engagement, and compensation, and then interpreting that data through a strategic lens, is the most strategic and data-driven way to manage talent.

The bottom line of engagement is this: Efforts to engage and retain an organization's most valuable talent should be highly personalized and have few limits. Conversely, those who are in nonpivotal roles, or who are low performing, low potential, and actively disengaged, should be removed from the organization.

Such a differentiated approach might be a departure for many HR leaders, but it's the key to finally moving the engagement needle in the direction of driving competitive advantage.

Review and Action Items

1. Too much time is spent on engagement of the entire workforce, and as a result this "peanut butter spreading" approach leaves too little for the few critical people who deserve and require more resources.

2. This chapter offers the provocative idea that after confirming talent who are high performing, high potential, and critical to the execution of organizational strategy, give them *anything*. Moving resources from the many low-performing, less pivotal, already disengaged employees takes courage but makes very strong business sense.

3. The limited number of engagement drivers is discussed, but extremely few leaders know which triggers to pull when trying to motivate their top talent. Unique drivers must be identified and delivered before pivotal talent will perform their best.

CHAPTER 10

HR TECHNOLOGY

HR Technology Comes of Age: Next-Generation Systems Bring New Usability, Efficiency to Talent Processes

Technology platforms designed for human resource functions have proved to be some of the least employee-friendly systems within the organization. Core platforms like the applicant tracking system (ATS), human resource management system (HRMS), and learning management system (LMS) are usually designed first with HR or training administrators in mind, and with the needs and preferences of line managers and employees taking a back seat. While these legacy platforms have pleased HR "superusers" with their record-keeping and compliance-related functions, they often leave line executives, employees, or job candidates frustrated with their clunky interfaces and lack of user-friendly features.

Yet as more workers outside the HR function begin to use these technologies for recruitment, analysis of workforce data, and self-service benefits administration, the stakes to ensure that these systems are as modern and easy to use as possible have risen.

Progressive CHROs and HRMS leaders have identified this technology gap and are investing in next-generation HR platforms with more intuitive, cloud-based interfaces, the latest artificial intelligence capabilities, expanded self-service tools, and more mobile-friendly functionality.

These leaders often arrange these technologies so they are delivered within shared services groups. These groups in turn increasingly seek offshoring and outsourcing opportunities to capitalize on labor arbitrage opportunities. The next step in the evolution of this business process cycle involves employing emerging technologies like robotic process automation (RPA) and blockchain to automate HR's operational and administrative tasks.

Although cost containment measures can drive compliance and reduce staff-related expenses, the best HR leaders use process changes as opportunities to reimagine how people are managed. The wave of new digital technologies including AI and machine learning will increasingly help CHROs and CEOs make smarter and faster talent decisions, which will be critical in rapidly changing business environments.

User Experience as the New "Nonnegotiable"

One recent industry survey found that the new "nonnegotiable" for HR technology buyers is the user experience. The study reported that compared with the previous year, 40 percent more respondents noted that *poor user experience was the primary reason for giving their current HR system vendors a low satisfaction rating.*[1]

There is a strong correlation between an exceptional user experience and high adoption rates of HR technology platforms by line clients. If platforms prove inefficient or frustrating to use, line executives, managers, and employees will simply go back to using spreadsheets, e-mail, or other legacy processes that are more welcoming because of their familiarity.

Technology-savvy CHROs and talent acquisition leaders also factor job candidates into the all-important user-experience equation. Interactions with HR improve when candidates can easily fill out job application forms or complete skills assessments from phones or tablets. Such improvements create less drop-off by high-quality candidates during what can be exasperating application processes.

Other tools like job applicant portals allow candidates to log on to pick their preferred interview times, to check their status in a hiring process, and even to get insight into a manager or team they might be working with.

Emerging Tech Delivers New Efficiencies

HR continues to be faced with a large amount of unstructured, resource-intensive work, primarily in the form of service requests arriving from employees via e-mail or phone calls. There also continue to be patterns of inefficiency and errors involved in HR data management and in the transfer of information from one system to another. Some CHROs and HRMS leaders are addressing these issues by investing in AI, chatbots, RPA, and other automated tools that help minimize the large volume of manual, rules-based work that needs to be performed within HR shared services groups. These new technologies can improve customer service provided to line clients by delivering answers to frequently asked questions faster and in more consistent fashion.

One study found that world-class HR groups spend 25 percent less and function with 30 percent less staff than average HR organizations, yet are more effective. These high-performing organizations have dramatically reduced staff that are assigned to transactional work.[2] Since HR often is expected to make operational improvements with a limited budget, employing the latest technologies can add administrative capacity and lower fixed labor costs over time.

Case Management and Robotic Process Automation Tools

Progressive HR teams are using tools like case management technology and RPA to address these issues. Case management allows HR to bypass e-mail requests or inquiries from employees and "auto-route" cases to the appropriate HR agent or team for follow-up. The technology adds efficiency to the process and usually results in more satisfied employees, as cases are more often routed to the right HR person and resolved faster and more effectively.

RPA—a technology common to finance, IT, and operations units— is making inroads in human resources by leveraging software bots that can take over or assist with manual tasks in payroll, benefits administration, recruiting, or onboarding. The technology is ideal for processes that involve collecting and entering data into systems, auditing data for integrity, performing basic calculations, and generating or distributing reports by aggregating data from multiple sources. RPA is designed to mimic the actions of humans if the steps are standard and linear. With the ability to perform the same process the same way every time, RPA also can ensure quality and consistency in data management. Some companies develop their own RPA bots, while others license them from established vendors.

Recent research from a global HR advisory firm found that 22 percent of the highest-performing HR organizations are currently implementing or have implemented RPA for use in HR, compared with just 6 percent of the lowest-performing organizations.[3]

Consider how RPA might be used in a healthcare recruiting scenario. At both the initial screening of candidates and again after a job offer is accepted, an RPA bot could automatically access and reference online databases to validate that a candidate has an active license to practice where the job is located. The bot also could download an electronic copy of the license and store it as part of the candidate's record in a recruiting application. This ability to automate the verification and storage steps adds speed and accuracy to the process.

RPA bots also can be used to trigger manual tasks, such as initiating the provisioning of a laptop based on a new-hire transaction or triggering a background check once an offer is accepted. After a hire, a bot could save an electronic offer letter as a PDF and export it to a vendor for secure off-site storage.

Evolution in HR Vendor Systems

For CHROs and HRMS leaders seeking to increase the adoption of HR technology platforms by their line clients, investing in more consumer-like, user-friendly systems has become a strategic priority. Technology vendors have taken notice of this demand, and many have released new cloud-based ATS and HRMS platforms featuring improved user interfaces, "mobile-first" designs, the latest AI capabilities, and tools that automate key HR workflows. The ATS has long been a technology that recruiters loved to hate. But as vendors gradually introduce new systems with more intuitive interfaces, collaborative capabilities, and automated workflow tools, modern systems have evolved into full-service recruiting platforms that integrate stand-alone applications such as skills assessments, employee referrals, onboarding, and candidate relationship management tools.

HRMS platforms have changed in the past few years as well. The early generations of these systems simply transformed paper processes to web-based forms that stored employee records, benefits data, and compensation structures in a single record system. These original technologies were primarily designed to deliver efficiency gains and often just enabled the collection of "bad data faster." But as the technology has grown smarter, it has helped talent leaders make more intelligent workforce decisions. Today's systems include such features as workforce management modeling and improved predictive analytics tools.[4]

Historically many HRMS platforms have had performance management processes and data at their center. Yet with so many companies dropping formal evaluations, there is an opportunity to abandon the rather questionable data entered by one's boss and replace it with insights that are gathered from more reliable and valid sources. This change will help overcome the garbage in, garbage out principle that remains prevalent in HR technology today.

Going forward, HR technologies as well as mature artificial intelligence tools should help talent leaders assess which of their pivotal employees might be most vulnerable to poaching by competitors in specific locations, or identify the best place to build new facilities or office space based on local talent pools. These technologies will also perform analyses across data sets to deliver actionable recommendations related to which of the most capable employees are most engaged, are most in need of time off, need a raise, or require use of other engagement drivers.

With these new improvements, HR technology is evolving from an obstacle to agile and effective talent management into an ally that aligns with business strategy. Although many organizations still have a way to go on the technology maturity curve, using new digital technologies and tools across the talent management spectrum will add heretofore unseen value and efficiency to HR processes.

THE FUTURE IS NOW
The Artificial Intelligence Revolution Comes to HR

Talent leaders now have at their disposal mature AI and machine learning technologies that can bring powerful new insights and laborsaving efficiencies to workforce planning, recruiting, employee engagement, learning and development, benefits administration, and other areas of HR.

Many of these tools have moved from experimentation to mainstream use in the human resources arena. More than half of HR managers (55 percent) believe AI will become a regular part of their function in the next five years, according to a recent study.[5]

Recruiters, for example, can now use AI to rapidly sift through volumes of LinkedIn profiles or résumés to identify those that best match job descriptions, saving precious time on the front end of the sourcing process. Many are using AI for "talent rediscovery," searching enormous databases of résumés in an ATS for candidates who've previously applied at an organization and still may be a good fit for open jobs. Other AI tools can gauge the facial expressions, word choices, or vocal tones of job candidates during videotaped interviews to gather more data in the selection process.

Corporate versions of Apple's Siri and Amazon's Alexa have also come to HR and are being used to answer frequently asked HR-related questions from employees or job candidates—a task that was previously assigned to HR service center representatives. These chatbots, or "virtual agents," are interactive software programs that can answer basic questions from employees or job applicants, using natural language processing to mimic human conversations. This frees up recruiters and HR staff for higher-value work. One global consulting company, for example, reported that a chatbot used in its talent development process answered more than 900,000 employee questions in its first two months of operation.[6]

AI also can be a boon for organizations that collect vast amounts of employee feedback through monthly or weekly pulse surveys, annual engagement surveys, internal social networks, and collaboration platforms. Many companies struggle with how to efficiently comb through this mountain of data and identify actionable insights that leaders can use to improve employee engagement and retention.

AI-driven sentiment analysis tools save time by helping HR professionals quickly find themes and trends in employee feedback. While such text analysis of survey responses isn't new, the emergence of smarter algorithms enables faster and more precise search and categorization of unstructured data like open-ended comments.

Review and Action Items

1. Nowhere in HR is change more rapid and exciting than in HR tech. The pace of evolution and integration of systems and platforms is finally catching up to the pace of change for technology in other business functions.

2. The HR tech evolution started with web-enabling paper forms that produced efficiencies but also produced "bad data faster." Solving for the GIGO principle requires that processes generating data be reex-

amined, and the mining of steps generating quality data must be front and center in process change.

3. Application of machine learning and artificial intelligence across HR processes is discussed, and obviously the adoption of these methods will mushroom in the near future. Safeguards must be in place to ensure that these efforts do not mislead data users into making decisions that are substandard or are in violation of labor laws in countries where employees reside.

PART 3

BRINGING IT ALL TOGETHER

CHAPTER 11

ROLE OF BOARDS

A t any company, the primary role of the board of directors is to provide oversight and strategic support for executive teams as they pursue their mission to create long-term shareholder value. The most important job within that charter is to select a CEO and oversee a sound succession management process for senior leadership roles in the company. Boards also have a responsibility to help management identify emerging risks and deal with unforeseen crises like data breaches, accounting scandals, or social media blunders.

One area where boards have an opportunity to make a greater impact on improving shareholder return is in their governance of smart talent strategies. In their book *Boards That Lead: When to Take Charge, When to Partner, and When to Stay Out of the Way*, Ram Charan, Dennis Carey, and Michael Useem identify situations where boards should take the lead and when they should partner with executive teams. The board should lead on selection of a chief executive officer; the identification and definition of the central idea of an organization; board architecture, competence, and its modus operandi; ethics and integrity issues; and compensation architecture.[1] Boards should partner with executive teams on strategy and capital allocation; talent development, financial goals, and shareholder value; risk appetite; resource allocation; and in the creation of a culture of decisiveness.

When should a board simply stay out of the way? Charan, Carey, and Useem suggest boards should give management a wide berth in the areas of execution, operations, delegation of executive authority, on nonstrategic decisions, and other areas excluded by a board charter.

Rethinking Total Shareholder Return

The top priority for most boards is delivering total shareholder return (TSR). TSR is a common language of any boardroom, and most CEOs are compensated on some variation of TSR, tied to how well they perform relative to competitors. While the traditional calculation of TSR will always be vital, more and more progressive leaders in the board effectiveness space have developed their own version of TSR, which has the goal of encouraging directors to place a stronger focus on the intersection of talent and strategy, an initiative that dovetails with a core principle of this book.

Carey, vice chairman and coleader of board services for Korn Ferry, has redefined TSR as *talent, strategy, and risk.* Carey believes that if boards do a good job of helping executive teams manage those three factors, it will naturally lead to delivering strong total shareholder return.

Because people create and execute strategy, it follows that without the right individuals in pivotal roles, the efforts of boards and executive teams to build traditional TSR become moot.

Boards should review and audit talent strategy in the same manner they do financial or operational strategies. They should help executive teams monitor succession management plans to ensure that promising talent is being identified early and carefully developed. They should make sure that their organization has the appropriate bench strength for pivotal roles.

A board also should partner with management to audit recruiting, development, compensation, and engagement processes to ensure that pivotal talent is being hired, nurtured, paid, engaged, and retained in ways that are superior to the competition's strategies in these areas. These forms of talent governance ensure a ready pipeline of talent to execute business plans with strength and consistency.

Talent and Leadership Versus the Compensation Committee

Robert Hallagan, vice chairman and coleader with Carey of Korn Ferry's Board Services practice, is another thought leader on the role of boards.

Hallagan has suggested that the compensation committee, a board sub-group, be renamed the "talent committee" to broaden its focus and emphasize the vital role that talent governance plays in business success.

The compensation committee of a public company board typically determines compensation targets and payouts for the four top officers of an organization as well as each board director. To broaden this group's impact, Hallagan suggests it not just review compensation but also audit the organization's talent practices to ensure they are best in class and operating in support of the business's direction. Hallagan believes this committee, and even the broader board, should spend as much as 30 percent of their time in meetings reviewing talent processes, metrics, and outcomes against predefined targets.

A good starting point for talent committees that are committed to getting beyond compensation issues for top officers would be for them to partner with executive teams on talent issues to review the three pillars of this book. Boards should:

- Ensure that talent strategy and processes of succession, engagement, compensation, culture, and leadership development are delivering long-term success on both definitions of TSR.
- Develop a scorecard to evaluate performance on an organization's talent strategy related to clear metrics. Aligned with the analytics maturity model detailed in Chapter 2, there should be high-quality data that demonstrate how efficient and effective an organization's human resources are in meeting financial and operational targets.
- Encourage CHROs to build talent strategies characterized by high-velocity, data-driven decision making and a more user-friendly talent process. This follows the notion that speed and simplicity are increasingly important for success across enterprise operating units.

A board also should hold executive teams accountable for creating an appropriate level of diversity and inclusion (D&I) in the organizations and customers they serve. D&I should permeate all talent processes and not be positioned as a stand-alone initiative. Companies should seek out new perspectives and diverse experiences of employees (and customers) who haven't historically been asked to provide input or were not traditionally perceived as potential leaders.

CEO Succession: Getting the Biggest Decision Right

The most important decision any board faces is choosing a company's CEO. Boards have a fiduciary duty to create good succession management practices in the organizations they oversee, and nowhere is that responsibility more important than in planning to replace the top executive.

Yet studies show that many boards are ill-prepared for this high-stakes decision, where a wrong choice can haunt companies for years and even decades. A study of the world's largest public companies found that organizations that do a poor job of planning for a CEO succession lose an average of $1.8 billion in shareholder value.[2]

That's an alarming statistic considering that the median tenure of a CEO in a Fortune 500 company is less than five years. Organizations have to replace their top executive with growing regularity, and many are using haphazard or suspect processes to do it.

Consider the fallout from poor CEO succession planning at companies like Hewlett Packard (HP) and Citigroup. After HP lost 40 percent of its market capitalization under new CEO Leo Apotheker, there were reports from an HP director that Apotheker had been "sold to the board" and that "it won't happen again." Apotheker's troubled reign lasted less than a year.[3] At Citigroup, chairman and CEO Sandy Weill had shunned or pink-slipped many of the top candidates to replace him during his tenure, including Jamie Dimon, who went on to remarkable success as CEO of JPMorgan Chase. Weill instead appointed friend Charles Prince to the CEO role, and he proceeded to lose billions of dollars from investing in bad debt. Prince was eventually replaced by Vikram Pandit, who himself exited shortly after, leaving behind stunned employees and a board scrambling to find another replacement.[4]

Contrast HP and Citigroup with the more strategic and data-driven succession process used at Ford Motor Co. when it hired Alan Mulally from Boeing to serve as its new CEO. When Ford's board began looking for a new CEO as it struggled with sliding market share and a looming banking crisis, it conducted a thorough search that led to hiring Mulally, who went on to lead a stunning turnaround at the company.

Before hiring Mulally, the Ford board had created a CEO "success profile," seeking a leader who was adept at breaking down silos to create a more unified global leadership team, who was well versed in complex operations and manufacturing, and who understood technology's role in sophisticated machinery. The board also wanted a CEO who was confident and indefatigable and who possessed experience turning around a struggling company. Mulally fit the bill on all counts, a hypothesis that proved to be true based on his successful tenure.[5]

But even high-performing boards can falter if they don't stay consistently focused on the principles and practices that align succession decisions with talent and business strategies. When Mulally eventually announced he was retiring, there wasn't panic in the ranks about who would replace him. That's because two years prior to his announcement, Ford had elevated Mark Fields to the role of chief operating officer and identified him as Mulally's heir apparent.

The board gave Fields day-to-day operations as part of a succession plan as he transitioned into the CEO job. Although Fields had his strengths, his strategy was never as clear as Mulally's, and he didn't move quickly enough to keep pace with emerging competitors in the ever-changing automotive sector. Some also believe Fields made the mistake of trying to fix what wasn't broken in Mulally's strategy. He was fired after three years at the helm of Ford.[6] Although Ford's board did well with the Mulalley transition, their process didn't work well at aligning business and talent strategies in the Fields (or as yet the Jim Hackett) appointments. This lack of alignment proved costly—four years after Mulalley's departure Ford market cap was cut by nearly 50 percent.

As the HP, Citigroup, and even Ford examples illustrate, placing the wrong person in the CEO role cripples performance, wounds brands, and sets organizations back for years. How to manage the extraordinary risk of replacing a CEO?

Start Early

"Succession planning needs to start long before a CEO announces he or she is leaving," says Bill George, Harvard Business School professor and the former CEO of Medtronic as well as former director on the boards of Goldman Sachs, Novartis, Target, and Exxon Mobil. "I have seen situations where the leading candidate for CEO fell out of favor, and shame on the company for only having one choice in its succession plan."

When I interviewed George, he explained that boards should insist on having active leadership development programs and should review their leadership bench strength a few times a year "Companies also need to ensure candidates fit the requirements of where the company is going in the future, not just where it's been in the past," he says.

A good succession plan should identify the names of at least seven CEO candidates at different levels of readiness. There should be:

- Two to three "near-ready" candidates working to polish and refine their short list of development goals.
- Another two to three candidates who won't be ready for a few years, and only then if they fill any significant gaps identified via senior leader assessments.
- Two to three long-range, high-potential candidates including diverse leadership talent from emerging markets. These long-range candidates should all score high on the seven signposts of superior leadership potential detailed in Chapter 6 on succession planning. These candi-

dates should undertake action learning experiences and other developmental exercises to prepare them for bigger P&L responsibilities.

All insider candidates should be developed through the use of challenging, enterprise wide assignments, as well as targeted development and coaching to close gaps between their capabilities and what will be required to lead the future enterprise. Rising leaders must be developed within the context of the business strategy, so that they can address real business challenges and opportunities while concurrently acquiring new skills.

Succession management also improves when a CEO takes a lead role in planning. Top executives hesitant to acknowledge the inevitability of their own departures will be roadblocks to the process. Boards should be assertive in ensuring that succession planning starts early and that CEOs aid in identifying a field of potential candidates.

Building a CEO Success Profile

Any CEO succession plan should be inextricably tied to business strategy. The first requires the creation of a CEO success profile that details four key dimensions needed for success—experiences, competencies, traits, and drivers—and ensures that each of these dimensions is defined and examined within the context of specific short- and long-term business imperatives agreed by the board's directors. When success profiles don't have deep roots in strategy, there is the danger of hiring one-size-fits-all "best athlete" who may take the business in the wrong direction. For example, if a strategy is tied to product innovation, operational excellence, or customer intimacy, candidates should possess the right capabilities in the four dimensional areas to execute those strategies at high levels. Strategic mindset, decision quality, and global perspective are examples of competencies that might be required. Experiences needed may include international assignments in targeted growth markets or, if demanded for a business to survive, a history of experiences directing organizational turnarounds while dealing with activist investors.

In one common scenario, the competencies and experiences of certain candidates might be a replica of the current CEO. Of course, there are times when following in the footsteps of experience of a successful incumbent makes sense. It is also increasingly likely in today's VUCA world that a totally different skillset is required to lead the pivot of a business away from its core when it's about to be disintermediated by the entrance of a new technology that threatens the organization's market position.

One area that's often overlooked in the success profiling step of the succession process is to require healthy drivers of a leader's motivation to develop and ascend the organizational chart. Directors can make incorrect assumptions about an individual's desire to progress into a senior executive role. Many mid- to high-level leaders find it risky to admit they are not striving for top jobs. Yet if organizations promote these individuals too quickly, they often discover they're not a good fit for a role with more pressure, responsibility, or ambiguity, and this can damage both the organization and the individual's career.

Unless succession planning takes a whole-person approach to assessing a candidate's capabilities and experiences while respecting his or her individual career interests, companies run the risk of investing in people who don't have the desire or motivation to advance into those next-level, mission-critical roles.

The complex personal traits and drivers that CEO candidates possess—who they are as people—are also vital aspects to include in success profiles. These traits determine how CEOs will deal with the inevitable challenges, ethical dilemmas, and interpersonal conflicts that arise on the job. Should candidates lack the right traits and drivers, it can easily derail their tenures.

Well-measured personal traits do a good job of predicting suspect or reckless behaviors that can derail an executive's career, endanger the business's brand, or jeopardize an organization's very survival. Ethical lapses in the top leadership ranks of organizations like Wells Fargo and Volkswagen underscore the importance of accurately gauging a potential successor's values, character, and integrity.

Wells Fargo CEO John Stumpf was forced to step down following a scandal where bank employees created millions of phony accounts without customers' knowledge. At Volkswagen, CEO Martin Winterkorn was jettisoned after an investigation showed that the German carmaker had manipulated the results of emissions tests. Winterkorn was replaced by internal candidate Matthias Müller. Müller was credited with steering the world's biggest carmaker through the emissions crisis and was reportedly making progress accelerating Volkswagen's efforts with electric and self-driving vehicles. Nonetheless, within three years of his appointment he was replaced by another internal executive, Herbert Diess. How Volkswagen, the largest carmaker in the world with $145 billion in revenue, could have three different CEOs in three years suggests that best practices in CEO succession are not commonplace.[7]

Similarly, it would have been interesting to see the psychological profile of Elizabeth Holmes, the founder and CEO of Theranos, who raised hundreds of millions of dollars from investors based on a $9 billion valuation, which made her the world's youngest self-made female billionaire. A few short years after settling a civil fraud lawsuit with the Securities and Exchange Commission related to misleading investors and the public about the state of its blood-testing technology, Theranos is near bankruptcy. Holmes has agreed to give up a chunk of her stock, has paid a $500,000 penalty, and is barred from serving as an officer or director in a public company for 10 years.

As illustrated in these three examples, aggregating each data point from the CEO assessment ensures that "gut feel" and extrapolation don't hold sway over validated science when evaluating CEO candidates. In addition, when board members make a strong interpersonal connection with a CEO candidate, the risk of using intuition to make choices grows and can lead to bad hires.

Traits and drivers also should align with a company's strategic direction. Companies in a start-up or turnaround mode might be tempted to favor a CEO candidate with deep knowledge of the industry, a good grasp of emerging trends, or elite subject-matter expertise. But if that candidate isn't comfortable with a high-visibility role and a need to constantly seek buy-in to a new vision, the board may find itself with a case of buyer's remorse.

Adding Rigor to CEO Candidate Assessment

To increase the odds of picking the right CEO successor, boards need to go beyond using garden-variety assessment methods when evaluating internal or external candidates. With internal candidates, boards will be appointing someone who may be holding the CEO job for the first time. The stakes in making the right call are high and warrant conducting due diligence in its most exacting form.

New assessment science can help boards make these predictions with far greater accuracy than before. The reality is that the assessment of CEO candidates in many organizations is still akin to having a 15-minute diagnostic discussion with a physician about a medical problem. Given the stakes, assessments should look more like a magnetic resonance imaging (MRI) test.

A whole-person, science-based assessment of CEO candidates has the rigor of an MRI. Evaluating candidates should be a multifaceted process that includes interviews with behavioral and industry experts, leadership simulations, psychometric measures, extensive exposure to a board, reference checks, and more. Insiders should be interviewed by a variety of leaders who have worked with the candidates to prevent favoritism, common biases, or boardroom politics. In fact, Bill George explains that paying for outside opinions combined with the rigor of multifaceted assessment keeps boards from making "a very costly mistake and keeps the candidate from signing up for a major career change that wouldn't be a good fit, and may end up in very visible failure."

Managing Risk

In an effort to explain why some leaders succeed where others fail, Lou Quast on behalf of Personnel Decisions International and the University of Minnesota conducted a study in 2011 consisting of 29,231 managers in the United States. He found that self-promoters, defined as managers who rated their own skills on a 360 survey as significantly higher than how others rated them, were six times more likely to derail.

Applying this insight to the notion of CEO blind spots when Apotheker was terminated from Hewlett Packard, I responded to a question from the *Wall Street Journal* that Apotheker lacked adequate "self-awareness around his limitations," and Apotheker responded accordingly, saying "I'm not perfect, and who is?"[8]

So how can organizations manage the extraordinary risk associated with CEO selection? Gather objective data to confirm or deny impressions and references on each candidate. In addition to interviews and psychometric measures assessments that simulate major CEO challenges can predict CEO readiness with extraordinary accuracy. The executive simulation results of Mullaly—among the best scores on record at Korn Ferry—proved predictive of his success not only as a Boeing executive but in leading the turnaround at Ford.[9]

In a recent longitudinal research study by Jeff Jones, Susanne Blazek, James Lewis, and Evelyn Orr, the researchers found further evidence that the type of CEO assessment methods we detailed in this chapter are a high predictor of a potential CEO's financial impact.[10] The researchers studied the performance and tenure of 188 public company CEOs over 16 years. They found that:

> Highest scoring CEOs on the assessment were 3.9 times more likely to deliver stronger financial performance than their five nearest industry competitors (the metrics used here were: market capitalization, stock price, revenue, earnings per share—EPS, total shareholder return—TSR, and earnings before interest, taxes, depreciation, and amortization—EBITDA). Of note: scores on the competency "strategic vision" had the biggest impact on an organization's market capitalization.

When compared to the lowest performing CEOs, the higher performing CEOs from the assessment had 30% longer tenure in the CEO role. The competencies that differentiated long vs. short tenure were customer focus, manages complexity, strategic vision, and aligns execution.

In the third and last step of the CEO succession planning process organizations must make the crucial decision of whether to opt for a "build" strategy (developing leaders from within) or "buy" approach (hiring externally) to fill the top leadership role. Boards should weigh internal versus external candidates using the same stringent assessment process to evaluate each candidate against a CEO success profile. Some additional factors should be considered in the build-versus-buy decision, such as the rapidity with which the CEO position needs to be filled or external forces that may require a new leader, from outside the organization, who is uniquely equipped to drive a specific strategy or to right a listing ship.

If building internal candidates is the choice, organizations should construct two succession plans. The first is a contingency plan designed for an unplanned exit by a CEO. Boards need to identify ready-now candidates in the event they have to move quickly to fill the job following a death, scandal, or other unanticipated departure.

The second plan is longer term and should identify at least three to four high-potential internal candidates to groom for succession to the CEO role over a period of time tied to the current CEO's expected departure. Those candidates should be assessed against a senior executive success profile and a development plan built to close talent gaps identified. For recommended strategies on how these leaders should be developed, see the section on leadership development in Chapter 5.

Developing a bench of well-prepared insiders is ideal, but some board members will prefer to hire CEOs from outside the organization. While that approach can prove effective—for example, Ford's hiring of Mulally from Boeing—it's typically the best option only in certain circumstances, such as when organizations are experiencing rapid growth or when a business model is under siege from disruptive competitors. It also can be a good option when succession candidates have been overshadowed for too long by the sitting CEO and the board couldn't get comfortable with any of the internal candidates as the number one executive.

If a decision is made to hire externally, boards should confidentially identify and evaluate a handful of executives from relevant industries, then conduct blind references to determine the top players. Finalist external candidates should then be assessed against the CEO success profile in the same rigorous fashion as internal candidates.

BEYOND THE HIRE
How to Support a New CEO

A newly hired CEO faces a breadth of challenges whether he or she is assuming the top job for the first time or is an experienced chief executive taking the helm of a new company. One of the best ways to ease that transition is to hire an executive coach (or in the case of Korn Ferry's Chief Executive Institute, use a team of four coaches, each focusing on one area of CEO mastery) to advise and counsel CEOs as they adapt to the new job.

But beyond the challenges of running a company also come threats to the CEO's physical and emotional well-being. Long workdays, constant travel, and unceasing pressure to outpace competitors can exact a toll—on CEOs as well as on their families—that workaholic executives often choose to ignore or that can go undetected.

Board support for new CEOs should include providing assistance that ensures these leaders maintain optimal energy and health to function at peak levels. Such support might also include financial planning advice, access to personal trainers or dietitians, transportation and security, and regular physicals with top medical providers. Concierge services also can help CEOs

(continued on next page)

manage the personal or family-related duties that often go unattended during frequent business travel or extended work hours.

Needs for such support vary widely by executive, so clear communication and trust between the board and CEO are critical to meet the needs of the new leader. To borrow a medical analogy, "Prescription of solution prior to diagnosis of the real need can lead to malpractice!"

Leading an organization only promises to grow more daunting as business models are disrupted by aggressive new competitors around the globe. Giving a new CEO all the support possible will help ensure he or she is able to meet those challenges and steer the organization on a path to success.

Acknowledging that onboarding support for new CEOs is a necessary but not sufficient condition for top team effectiveness is another secret of success. Ignoring the changes in the top team dynamic that a new CEO introduces is a guaranteed way to paralyze an otherwise successful executive committee. In order to get beyond new leader assimilation and onto high performance the executive team needs to reestablish its purpose (do they exist only to inform one another of their activities, or are they a body that will align on decisions, then execute as an interdependent team?), ensure they have complementary capabilities, establish decision making processes, rules, and roles, and agree on ways to hold each other accountable for results over time. A new CEO who is but one of the participants in this group is likely to need help ironing out these kinks soon after arrival.

Avoiding a "Roomful of Strangers"

How board directors interact and build chemistry with one another is also critical to their success, particularly when the organizations they oversee encounter a crisis. As former CEOs and senior leaders, board members are accustomed to getting their own way and having the bucks stop at their desks. In this new scenario of working with other "alphas," they often have to figure out—some for the first time in their careers—a different style of influence than the one that got them to the CEO job in their own company.

Given the mix of personalities, varied areas of expertise, and the fact that boards only convene a few times a year, there is a threat that boards are really a "roomful of strangers." Such a development can be dangerous, especially when boards face high-stakes decisions during a crisis and it's important they move quickly to reach consensus.

"There is an elusive thing on boards called chemistry," says George. "You can check all of your governance boxes, but if you don't have the right chemistry among your board members, things will not usually go well."

George knows firsthand the importance of building strong board relationships. As a member of the Goldman Sachs board during the subprime mortgage crisis, George and his board colleagues were faced with momentous decisions that needed to be made on tight timelines.

"The board was under enormous pressure, and since we were based all over the world, it was hard for us to gather in one place," George told me in our interview. "We had big decisions to make quickly, such as whether to take an equity investment from Warren Buffett or become a bank holding company. These were decisions with huge long- term consequences, and if we didn't have the chemistry on the board that had been built up over a 10-year period, it could have been a disaster."

Directors are given board effectiveness surveys each year, a requirement for publicly traded firms. But those assessments are usually perfunctory and tied solely to compliance and legal matters. It's important that board members get a deeper insight into one another's decision-making styles and personality differences. That's because there is typically a mix of risk avoiders and risk takers, extroverts and introverts, and varied thinking styles on any given board.

In addition to required annual governance audits, the best way to gain these insights is through a formal, qualitative assessment of each director, who then receives confidential feedback about his or her leadership and thinking style. A composite drawn from all director assessments reveals the tendencies of the entire board, as well as defines the spectrum of traits and behaviors. This can help to clearly define the roles of all board members by evaluating the tendencies they will display that distinguish and differentiate them from other directors in both positive and potentially negative ways.

Such an assessment helps board members develop a better understanding of themselves and how to work more effectively with their equally strong-ego board colleagues. When they understand their own traits and drivers relative to those of the other directors, it usually gets them to high performance faster than a roomful of strangers would.

Reflecting on the impact of this type of board evaluation, Mike Marberry, CEO of JM Huber, observed, the consulting Korn Ferry did with the JM Huber board afforded them an opportunity to "have more individual interaction among board members prior to board meetings, and caused us as a group to think more about the agenda, how the agenda gets set, and to make sure that we're sensitive to different perspectives and drivers among our board members so we're focusing on the right things to meet critical needs."

George said board members with good chemistry often invest considerable time in getting to know one another, in some cases by taking trips together, such as one taken by the members of a board he was on to meet with venture capitalists in Silicon Valley.

"You need to take time to get to know each other as human beings," George said. "You don't get to know someone's personal side when you only see them in meetings. I think boards need to do that as much as any executive team does. Building that chemistry will pay off when facing difficult times together."

As businesses continue to get hit with the inevitable challenges and crises, such as a data breach, unethical behavior by senior leaders, activist investors, environmental accidents, or accounting scandals, it's becoming increasingly important for board members to work well together to help executive teams steer through those difficulties.

By gaining insights into how fellow board members think and operate, directors build trust and improve their ability to handle these challenges. Boards that are skilled at managing disasters also are more effective at driving their companies to higher levels of performance as they apply those skills to help senior leaders allocate capital, mitigate risk, plan CEO succession, and enhance diversity and inclusion. These accomplishments are all difficult for boards to achieve until the members have greater insight into one another's leadership and thinking styles.

Review and Action Items

1. The critical role of board oversight in talent processes is discussed. Recommendations are made for how to reexamine the intersection of talent, strategy, and risk (the "new TSR") in relation to total shareholder return. Boards are encouraged to expand the role, charter, and agenda of the compensation committee.
2. CEO succession process steps and methods for mitigating risk and increasing success are discussed. CEO successes—and some spectacular failures of companies that did not follow these critical steps in their CEO transition process—are shared.
3. Opportunities for boards to role-model alignment of talent and governance strategies are discussed. Important challenges related to getting directors aligned are shared, and parallels to executive team alignment and high performance are made.

CHAPTER 12

THE TALENT WALTZ

The Critical Alignment

In evaluating whether an organization is operating at the intersection of strategy and talent, CEOs, CHROs, executive teams, and even boards of directors confront two high-stakes questions:

1. Are all talent processes aligned with one another in a manner that most effectively and efficiently delivers necessary talent to the business?
2. Is there are a measurable impact of these processes on the execution of business imperatives?

In far too many cases, the answer to both questions is no. A disconcerting 83 percent of CHROs express concern that their organizations do not possess the talent needed to deliver on strategic priorities, according to Korn Ferry research.[1]

This is troubling news. Organizations' talent strategies must be aligned with their business strategies for companies to thrive. This alignment also needs to be recalibrated when strategic shifts occur— and these shifts are taking place with growing regularity. A majority of executives expect to see more divestitures in the coming months, according to *CFO* magazine.[2] Merger and acquisition activity is on track to reach the highest number of consolidations on record, according to the *Wall Street Journal* and data provider Dealogic.[3] Chief executives and CHROs in more than 80 percent of companies must quickly align their talent and their business strategies, Korn Ferry research shows.[4]

The cover of the July/August 2015 issue of *Harvard Business Review* featured an illustration of a bomb with a lighted fuse and the headline, "It's Time to Blow Up HR and Build Something New. Here's How."[5] The articles inside have titles and subtitles such as "Rethinking Human Resources," "Why We Love to Hate HR," and "A New Role for the CHRO." Leading HR experts are not the only groups intensifying their focus on HR's purpose and talent management purview. In recent years, CEOs have thrust talent to the top of their priority lists. For the second year in a row, chief executives who participate in the Conference Board's annual survey of CEO concerns hold up human capital as their top challenge.[6]

This book was written to answer the growing calls for a major rethinking of enterprise talent strategy. A fundamental challenge—and an invaluable strategic opportunity—confronting CEOs and CHROs is to establish strong alignment between enterprise and talent strategy. This book presented three principles that guide the redevelopment of talent processes that optimize organizational performance. This final chapter summarizes and simplifies steps that help organizations to drive strategic change and performance results and to place the right talent more swiftly into the right roles. It is expected, then, that this carefully selected talent will design and execute strategies that deliver sustainable competitive advantage. Getting all the parts in place is difficult work, given the prevalence of deep-rooted obstacles, four of which are examined at the conclusion of this chapter.

Much of the focus in this chapter is on the relationship between the CEO and the CHRO, but all leaders in an organization must lean in to maximize results.

If this effort is delayed, the strategy-talent gap will only widen. The problem—and it is pervasive—is that too few companies have the right talent in the right place, and as a result, their growth engines misfire. Organizations could, instead, better find and funnel talent into the right places if their organizational and talent strategies were tightly synced.

Three Steps to Talent-Strategy Alignment

To get their organizational and talent strategies in line, leaders need to take three comprehensive, straightforward steps. But the direct nature of these activities belies how rarely they are present in many organizations. That's because these steps are difficult to execute and tough to sustain in the face of ingrained organizational habits and tendencies. If any one of these steps is neglected or performed inadequately, alignment will not occur. Because there are three steps and because the order of execution is critical to success, this model is called the "Talent Waltz." Repeating these steps over and over, just like the dance, is the way to operate at the intersection of strategy and talent.

Step 1: The CEO and CHRO Define Specific Talent Requirements for Successful Strategy Execution

This process identifies the essential talent building blocks—organizational culture, decision-making and governance operations, performance metrics, incentive structures, talent pools, and related capabilities—required to deliver on performance objectives.

The CEO and CHRO must start by detailing how the business will beat its competitors and capture its share of the addressable market that it is seeking. Is the company investing in organic growth opportunities or seeking to scale through mergers and acquisitions? Does innovation, globalization, or digitization define the strategy? Each approach requires unique capabilities. For example, if a company is driving innovation, it needs a robust research and development function, more internal collaboration, and an organizational culture that rewards experimentation without punishing failure. Another company focused on global expansion must obtain international leadership experience and cross-cultural management capabilities at a world-class level.

Strategically aligned talent requirements should be agreed across a leadership team, as sacrifices will need to be made. Organizations cannot be great at everything and must pick their "must-win" areas. One study of 1,600 U.S. companies in the book *Talent Wins* reported that "companies that reallocated financial capital aggressively from one division to another, based on market opportunity and performance, were worth 40 percent more after fifteen years than companies that had been relatively passive."[7]

The same is true for reallocating talent to optimize performance. But relatively few leadership teams or boards devote sufficient attention to talent strategy during their quarterly and annual off-site planning meetings. Strategic and annual operation plans are covered in detail, but too often talent discussions are given short shrift and abbreviated on the corporate agenda.

The CEO and CHRO also must curate the optimal structure for the organization to operate in, the decision-making and governance processes that will deliver strong performance, the incentives that reward performance, and the type of organizational culture that brings all this to life. Once these larger structural and cultural considerations are addressed, leaders should ask the following more HR-specific questions:

- Given our business strategy, which roles are most pivotal to its execution, and how should these roles be organized?
- In those roles, what specific competencies, experiences, traits, and drivers are required for success?
- What are the employee value propositions for these roles?
- How urgent are these talent needs?

Note that urgency is important because it will help determine the methods (e.g., leadership development, hiring) to address talent gaps as presented in step 3 in this Talent Waltz.

Consider how this urgency might affect a cable company whose strategy is to grow by increasing market share among subscribers. After assessing their industry's ferociously competitive environment in which some customers may be tempted to flee their current providers, the CEO and her executive team determine that constant connectivity is the competitive differentiator. They realize that customer satisfaction and retention hinges on the Internet, televisions, and phones working every time a customer uses them. This leads them to scrutinize their company's customer service area, the critical nature of the function's leadership roles, the organizational culture of the company, performance management processes, incentive structures, and talent. They focus on identifying what steps are needed to ensure that this area has the right leadership, culture, and talent processes. This talent profile helps the organization hire and develop the best service executives in the industry, build the best customer service, and allocate a disproportionate amount of resources to this area.

The previously unglamorous, and quite possibly underresourced, customer services and many call center employees' now become a critical driver of strategy.

Although few would disagree with this approach, it often falls short for the following reasons:

- The CHRO may not understand the strategy well enough to analyze the capabilities it needs.
- The CHRO may be excluded altogether from this type of strategic planning, instead working through an intermediary, such as the chief operating officer, due to reporting relationships.
- Embarking on this analysis requires the entire leadership team to accept a subsequent need for radical changes.
- Big-budget, deeply entrenched recruiting programs championed by influential executives may need to be shelved in favor of more strategically appropriate, focused programs.
- A willingness to commit to potentially major changes—emptying out corporate headquarters to support international growth, for example—may not be present.
- The treatment of certain organizational roles as more valuable runs counter to a longstanding HR tendency toward the equitable treatment of all employees.

Step 2: The CEO and CHRO Assess the Current Talent Capabilities Versus the Organization's Strategic Needs

Once the leaders have identified roles and needed capabilities in their organization and methodically organized them into more specific competencies, experiences, traits, and drivers, they can compare the talent needs with the organization's inventory baseline of talent. They must conduct a comprehensive assessment and ask the following questions about what's working and what's not:

- Which individuals are delivering strong results and demonstrating the behaviors required for strong performance in pivotal areas of strategy execution?
- How strong is the pipeline of talent who can one day backfill the most strategic roles: who has longer-term potential, who might be ready for a near-term bigger assignment, and do we have enough of these individuals in the right places?
- How strong is the culture today at enabling the people and processes most critical to the organization's success?
- How well do the reward and recognition systems work in motivating the right people to do the right things?
- Are these roles designed and organized in a way that maximizes performance?

The CEO and CHRO aren't looking at just their organization's current talent but also their likely future hires. This process applies to all pivotal roles and talent pools in all levels of the organization as they were identified in the first step of the waltz. The identification and comparisons of talent inside and outside of an organization is the only way to know whether an organization has the best talent in the world in positions where they can make the biggest impact on strategy

The work frequently bogs down here because the assessment of existing talent relies too heavily on notoriously inaccurate and biased processes. Business-line executives and managers may lack a framework and terminology to evaluate and discuss their talent in a consistent way, and it is understandably hard for managers to objectively evaluate their people. Their assessments usually overvalue results accomplished while neglecting what an individual might achieve in the future with the right support. Performance review politics also hinder assessments of current talent: "I'm not going to challenge Steve's rosy evaluation of his top lieutenant, because if I do, he might challenge the plum rating I gave my top lieutenant."

A lack of common evaluation criteria—and, especially, a lack of data on performance, potential, and readiness to handle new challenges—is a common obstacle too. Where data does exist, it often has little value in predicting current or future performance outcomes. Finally, performance assessments may not measure individuals against success profiles (i.e., the organization measures the wrong indicators). Fixing these data problems is essential to the Talent Waltz. Principles for systemic fixes are outlined in Part 1 of this book, and examples of how many companies have overcome these problems are reported throughout Part 2.

Step 3: The CEO and CHRO Craft a Strategy to Close Gaps Between the Current Talent Pool and the Business's Strategic Needs

After undertaking the previous steps, leaders must now design a talent management plan. HR should identify which roles can be filled internally and which roles require external recruiting. Some may be filled by redeployment of existing talent. This assessment should be based on data at the individual and organizational level. When HR looks at all the data, it also should draw conclusions about gaps in current recruiting, promotion, development, engagement, inclusion, and reward programs.

Timing also becomes a crucial consideration in this effort, as CEOs are under intense pressure to make and successfully execute strategic shifts. Knowing this, CHROs must act with the appropriate urgency, striking the right balance between actions focused on the immediate acquisition of external talent and those emphasizing the development of internal talent. When the urgency is great, CEOs and CHROs need to make tough calls swiftly about buy-versus-build talent approaches.

The sound execution of this gap-filling step can be decisive in determining if an organization successfully aligns its business and talent strategies. I have seen companies and their HR departments do excellent work on the first two phases of the waltz only to drop the ball on step 3. That's because organizations often lack the will to execute the changes needed to get the right talent into the right roles.

These changes routinely affect almost all major talent management processes, including sourcing, recruiting, onboarding, training, leadership development, succession planning, performance management, engagement, and compensation.

As a result, this step can be the most difficult to carry out and sustain. Successful execution requires a clear vision of how existing talent management processes and approaches must change, the leadership courage needed to make the changes, and the stamina to sustain the efforts over the long haul. Indeed, stamina and leadership courage are required to reallocate HR budgets, time, and roles, which is almost always necessary.

CASE STUDY

Johnson & Johnson

Founded in 1886, Johnson & Johnson (J&J) is a medical device, pharmaceutical, and consumer healthcare products company. The corporation includes some 250 subsidiary companies with operations in 60 countries and products sold in over 175 countries. Recently, Johnson & Johnson has seen worldwide sales of $76 billion, and its market capitalization has grown more than twice as fast as the Dow 30 or S&P 500 index over the past 30 years. Critical to its success is a firm commitment to be of high quality in "everything we do." Given this, it is no wonder that its talent practices are the envy of many and are often bench-

marked by other organizations. I recently spoke with Sarah
Brock, global head of assessment and development, to get her
perspective on the three principles in *The Talent Manifesto* and
how they are represented in the J&J talent processes.

Strategy

To capitalize on best practices realized from decentralized
corners of the organization and to capture cost synergies of its
large global footprint, an approach the company terms "One
J&J" was recently built that has rationalized many business
processes. Many talent strategies also align with the One J&J
direction in that they've helped the businesses create a leaner
organizational structure, they've created global shared services
for the more transactional work, and they've driven standardization for certain processes and experiences, including how the
businesses identify their pivotal talent. J&J businesses understand the criticality of managing their pivotal talent very carefully, and they are focused on driving innovation by attracting
and retaining the world's top talent in R&D, commercial general
management, and other roles.

Data

Five years ago, J&J ramped up its efforts to create data-based
insight on top leaders. Although confident it was managing talent strategically, the company wanted to go from "we think" to
"we know." In order for its businesses to continue to prosper,
J&J needed to increase confidence that it had the best talent in
the world across the top of the organization and particularly in
pivotal roles.

   Brock, an industrial psychologist herself, along with other
data scientists, created a world-class assessment process where
competencies, experiences, and other drivers relating to leader-

(continued on next page)

ship and innovation were quantified using interviews, psychometrics, and business simulations. The process helps J&J businesses to assess internal and external candidates to see who is best for a given senior role. J&J's efforts didn't stop there. To ensure it had the best talent in the world, it prepared external benchmarks of leaders in companies that were touted by *Forbes* and *Fortune* to be among the most innovative in the world. Using data from assessments of all candidates and comparing results to leaders from the highest-performing benchmark companies, J&J businesses confidently hired with "eyes wide open." These tools also helped J&J companies to assess how their own business cultures could better support and recognize innovation, better enabling the leaders who assessed as real innovators to thrive.

J&J now can better identify the persons who can drive innovation in pivotal roles. It can better support top talent to succeed like never before in delivering the innovation that its businesses require for continued success. Further, it has built upon what it has learned about innovation and has cascaded those learnings down to additional organizational levels, changing how its businesses identify and develop the talent needed to ensure that growth is delivered by people generating new ideas for generations to come.

And the User Experience?

Brock shared with me that it simply was not an option to roll out a new process at J&J without great science and real simplicity. Partnering with Korn Ferry throughout this journey, Brock requested our team to take a two-day process that was always delivered in person and, without losing any of the validity, deliver J&J assessments virtually, often on short notice, in an interactive experience lasting just a few hours—anywhere in the world.

After assessing more than 1,000 senior leaders, we found:

- That 92 percent of the participants surveyed said the assessment was engaging
- That 89 percent said the assessment provided value, focus, and useful strategies for development
- That 88 percent of manager responses said the assessment provided value or insight to them

---

Obstacles to Overcome

CHROs must spearhead the work described above, grappling with common obstacles from numerous sources, exerting their influence. To succeed they must sway the CEO, the board, the rest of the executive team, and the business-line leaders. This effort is crucial, especially to overcome four of the most typical stumbling blocks:

- **LOST IN TRANSLATION.** Business-line executives struggle to translate their talent needs into specific capabilities to guide HR departments in hiring and development practices. That's because the managers lack objective criteria and reliable data to do so. In many cases, organizations also lack a common language for talking about talent and its alignment with organizational strategy. Talent frameworks like Korn Ferry's Four Dimensions of Leadership and Talent (see Figure 12.1) and methodologies can help address this challenge.

  At the board level, the directors' general questions about talent strategies fail to get translated into concrete action. A prescription for how boards can take a more active role in governance of talent processes is outlined in Chapter 11. There is a procession of survey data showing that talent ranks as the number one CEO concern—so what is our talent strategy? Board members can dig deeper. While many directors ask if succession plans exist at a company's highest level, fewer ask more extensive questions or utilize scorecards tracking the relationship between succession moves and strategy execution. ·

FIGURE 12.1 Korn Ferry's Four Dimensions of Leadership and Talent: competencies, experiences, traits, and drivers

Competencies

Skills and behaviors required for success that can be observed.

FOR EXAMPLE:

Decision quality, strategic mindset, global perspective, and business insight.

Experiences

Assignments or roles that prepare a person for future opportunities.

FOR EXAMPLE:

Functional experiences, international assignments, turnarounds, and fix-its.

WHAT YOU DO

– –

WHO YOU ARE

Traits

Inclinations, aptitude, and natural tendencies a person leans toward, including personality traits and intellectual capacity.

FOR EXAMPLE:

Assertiveness, risk taking, confidence, and aptitude for logic and reasoning.

Drivers

Values and interests that influence a person's career path, motivation, and engagement.

FOR EXAMPLE:

Power, status, autonomy, and challenge.

- **LEADERSHIP COURAGE LACKING.** Creating and managing an effective talent strategy requires tough decisions. Many CHROs and HR departments would benefit by amassing more experience negotiating, influencing, and persuading boards and executive colleagues that their organization must make difficult but strategically beneficial talent decisions. Filling gaps between the talent required for the business strategy and the company's talent profile is akin to zero-based budgeting: "This year, we're doing away with all talent programs that do not directly align with the changes in our must-win objectives." It takes courage to challenge the status quo; to face off against the influential executive who championed the leadership development program that costs $5 million annually but adds little strategic value; and to take money from one part of the organization so the company can hire 200 of the best and brightest service technicians. Such displays of courage, however, are critical steps in the journey to top performance.

- **BENCHMARKING BIAS.** Too many organizations by default rely on talent strategies that amount to copycat versions of other leading companies' HR practices. Benchmarking can be an effective tool, but it should not substitute for a company creating its own talent strategy that addresses its unique needs. Talent management practices that succeed at one company are not necessarily best practices for all organizational cultures; they work well for a specific company because the talent activities align with its business strategies. These "best practices" also work well because the benchmark company puts them in place in concert with many other related processes—and all of these align with its unique strategy.

- **CEO-CHRO CALIBRATION.** Organizational knowledge and familiarity are crucial components when CEOs and CHROs seek to align the business and talent strategies. This is especially true given the difficulty of making major changes at all levels of the enterprise. Newly hired CHROs, including those brought in by CEOs to make changes, can move more quickly than is prudent and, as a result, encounter more resistance and less support. Newly hired CEOs brought in to implement new strategies, similarly, may move too quickly for the existing CHRO; this gives rise to the same resistance and support problems. Getting alignment on talent priorities may take some time, but when done well, execution is accelerated because the impact of talent on results is broadly understood.

Conclusion

When operating at the intersection of strategy and talent, the CEO and CHRO need to calibrate their thinking on the speed and magnitude of change. This need is widespread; on the basis of fieldwork and research, I estimate that the likelihood that a CEO and CHRO are aligned on all three steps in the Talent Waltz is less than 20 percent. Strategy-talent execution requires CEO-CHRO alignment. It also requires action. Delaying the interrelated steps in this chapter would defy the principles of *The Talent*

Manifesto. This in turn is a recipe for failure that puts strategy execution, financial performance, and likely many jobs—including your own—at great risk.

Review and Action Items

1. In this summary chapter the concept of the Talent Waltz was introduced. Any waltz will have three steps, which must be taken in order. And then the order is repeated: 1-2-3, 1-2-3, etc. The Talent Waltz is a key part of the manifesto, as it articulates the three steps and the order in which they must be taken.

2. The first step in the waltz answers the question "What quality and quantity of talent is needed to execute our business strategy and beat our competitors?" The response must address structural and cultural factors, must identify the talent most pivotal to execution, and must define the competencies, experiences, traits, and drivers for people in each pivotal role.

3. The second step of the waltz is to evaluate people and culture against the target that was defined in step 1. Gut reactions are not good enough; reliable and valid measures of talent are needed to baseline current versus desired capabilities in order to avoid costly mistakes.

4. The final waltz step is to identify the most effective and efficient ways to close gaps identified between waltz steps 1 and 2. Possibilities include developing talent from within an organization to fill gaps over time, hiring outside talent to fill gaps more quickly, and partnering with or purchasing other organizations to fill critical talent gaps.

NOTES

Introduction

1. Mark Perry, "Fortune 500 Firms 1955 v. 2017: Only 60 Remain, Thanks to the Creative Destruction That Fuels Economic Prosperity," AEI.org, October 20, 2017.

Chapter 1

1. Aaron Pressman, "Can AT&T Retrain 100,000 People?," *Fortune*, March 2017.
2. Ibid.
3. Groysberg and Connolly, "The Three Things CEOs Worry About the Most," *Harvard Business Review*, 2015.
4. The Conference Board, 2016.
5. Jen Wieczner, "The New Geek Squad (That's Fixing Best Buy)," *Fortune*, November 2015.
6. Deloitte's Global Human Capital Trends survey, 2017.
7. John. W. Boudreau and Peter Ramstad, *Beyond HR: The New Science of Human Capital*, Harvard Business School Press, 2007.
8. Boyce, et al., *Journal of Organizational Behavior*, Volume 36, Issue 3, April 2015, pages 339-359.
9. Deloitte's Global Human Capital Trends survey, 2017.

Chapter 2

1. "Becoming a People Company," Sage People, 2017 survey report.
2. 2016 study on talent analytics and measurement, Lighthouse research.
3. Deloitte's Global Human Capital Trends study, 2017.
4. "2014–2015 HR Systems Industry Survey," Sierra-Cedar.
5. R. J. Heckman, "Getting to Strategic Talent Management Analysis" presentation, PDI Ninth House Research, 2008.
6. Edward E. Lawler III and John W. Boudreau, "Effective Human Resource Management: A Global Analysis," 2012.
7. "2017 Performance Management Study," Mercer.

8. "2015–2016 HR Systems Industry Survey," Sierra-Cedar.
9. John W. Boudreau and Peter Ramstad, *Beyond HR: The New Science of Human Capital*, Harvard Business School Press, 2007.
10. "Managing Performance Data for Business Advantage," Korn Ferry case study.
11. PwC's 2017 Global HR Technology Survey 2017.

Chapter 3

1. Jeff Gothelf, "How HR Can Become Agile (and Why It Needs to)," *Harvard Business Review*, June 2017.
2. "What Is Jeff Bezos's Day 1 Philosophy?," *Forbes*, April 2017.
3. Diane Gherson, "Does Remote Work Hinder Innovation?," SHRM, October 2017.
4. Aaron Pressman, "Can AT&T Retrain 100,000 People?," *Fortune*, March 2017.
5. Roy Maurer, "GE's Move into Digital Necessitated 'Blitzscale' Hiring," SHRM, December 2016.
6. Dave Zielinski, "Few HR Tech Platforms Untouched by Mobile Trend," SHRM, December 2016.
7. Valerie Bolden-Barrett. "Salesforce Drops $6M to Close Gender Pay Gap," *HR Dive*, September 2017.
8. Deloitte's Global Human Capital Trends survey, 2015.
9. Valerie Bolden-Barrett. "Home Depot rolls Out Interview Self-Scheduling to Fill More than 80K Openings," *HR Dive*, February 2018.

Chapter 4

1. Peter Cappelli and Anna Tavis, "The Performance Management Revolution," *Harvard Business Review*, October 2016.
2. Deloitte's Human Capital Trends survey, 2017.
3. "Performance Management: Moving from Theory to Practice," 2017 external benchmark study, Korn Ferry Hay Group.
4. David Rock, Beth Jones, and Camille Inge, "Reengineering Performance Management: How Companies Are Evolving PM Beyond Ratings," NeuroLeadership Institute, 2015.
5. Laszlo Bock, *Work Rules! Insights from Inside Google That Will Transform How You Live and Lead*, Hachette Book Group, 2015.
6. Erica Bank,"Reinventing Performance Management at Deloitte," Insights, Association for Talent Development, January 13, 2016.
7. Dana Wilkie, "Is the Annual Performance Review Dead?," SHRM.org, August 2015.

Chapter 5

1. Aaron Pressman, "Can AT&T Retrain 100,000 People?," *Fortune*, March 2017.

2. Ibid.
3. Deloitte's Global Human Capital Trends survey, 2017.
4. Naomi Eide, "Reskilling Crisis Emerging as 1.4m Jobs Face Technology Disruption," *HR Dive*, 2018.
5. Deloitte's Global Human Capital Trends survey, 2017.
6. Michael Beer, "The Great Training Robbery," research paper, 2016.
7. "Leaders for a Digital Transformation," Korn Ferry report, 2016.
8. David Dolitch, Kevin Cashman, and Desi Kimmins, "Leadership Development: CEO's Strategic Powerhouse," Korn Ferry white paper, 2015.
9. Ibid.
10. "The Future of Jobs," World Economic Forum.
11. Andrew Palmer, "Lifelong Learning Is Becoming an Economic Imperative," *Economist*, 2017.
12. "Corporate Learning Insider Report," joint study by LinkedIn and Whiteboard Advisors, 2017.
13. Roy Mauer, "Closing the Looming Health Care Talent Gap," SHRM, 2017.
14. "Lowe's Takes Another Step to Win Workers in a Tight Labor Market," CNBC, 2018.
15. Cade Metz, "Tech Giants Are Paying Huge Salaries for A.I. Talent," *New York Times*, October 22, 2017
16. Arnold, Jennifer, "How to Adopt Skills-Based Hiring Practices," SHRM Online, February 2018.
17. "2016–2017 HR Systems Survey," Sierra-Cedar.
18. Josh Bersin, "The Disruption of Digital Learning: Ten Things We Have Learned," Bersin on joshbersin.com, March 2017.
19. Mike Prokopeak, "Measurement, Meet Management," *Chief Learning Officer*, March 7, 2018.
20. Rachel Silverman, "So Much Training, So Little to Show for It," *Wall Street Journal*, October 26, 2012.
21. Gurdjian, Pierre, Halbeisen, Thomas, and Lane, Kevin. 2014. °Why Leadership Development Programs Fail," McKinsey & Company.
22. Patti Phillips, Jack Phillips, and Rebecca Ray, "Measuring the Success of Leadership Development," Association for Talent Development (ATD), July 2015.

Chapter 6

1. "Succession Matters: Effective Succession Management Planning," Korn Ferry Institute, 2015.
2. Deloitte's Global Human Capital Trends survey, 2016.
3. "Succession Matters: Accurate Identification of Leadership Potential," Korn Ferry Institute, 2015.
4. Ibid.
5. Ibid.

6. "Succession Matters: Effective Succession Management Planning," Korn Ferry Institute, 2015.
7. Ibid.
8. "Succession Matters: Impactful Leadership Development and Accelerated Readiness," Korn Ferry Institute, 2015.

Chapter 7

1. Tom McMullen, Mark Royal, and Dow Scott, "Retention of Key Talent and the Role of Rewards," *WorldatWork Journal*, 2012.
2. Joint research study from the Korn Ferry Hay Group, WorldatWork, and Loyola University, 2012.
3. WorldatWork 2016–2017 Salary Budget Survey.
4. "The Real Gap: Fixing the Gender Pay Divide. A Gender Pay Gap Exists—Just Not in the Way Conventional Wisdom Holds," Korn Ferry study, 2016.
5. Ibid.
6. Laszlo Bock, *Work Rules! Insights from Inside Google That Will Transform How You Live and Lead,* Hachette Book Group. 2015.
7. Ibid.
8. Ibid.
9. Tom McMullen and Katie Lemaire, "Differentiating Pay Without Performance Ratings," *Workspan*, June 2016.
10. Tom McMullen, "Five Things I've Learned About Rewards Communications," *Workspan*, July 2012.

Chapter 8

1. D. Ciampa, "Almost Ready: How Leaders Move Up," *Harvard Business Review*, January 2005.
2. "Hay Group Study Finds Employee Turnover in Retail Industry Is Slowly Increasing," Korn Ferry Hay Group, May 2012.
3. Christina Merhar, "Employee Retention—The Real Cost of Losing an Employee," Zane Benefits, Peoplekeep.com, February 4, 2016.
4. Bryne Mulrooney, Bill Gilbert, Jan Mueller, and Neil Griffiths, "The Talent Forecast: Hire with a Purpose," Korn Ferry Institute, March 8, 2017.
5. Ibid.
6. Korn Ferry case study, 2016.
7. E. S. Blazek, J. Jones, J. Lewis, and E. Orr, "Leading Indicators: Ensuring the Right Mix of a CEO's Competencies Can Result in Longer Tenures, and Play a Key Role in How Organizations Are Led," *Proof Point*, Korn Ferry, 2015.
8. Mulrooney, Gilbert, Mueller, and Griffiths, "The Talent Forecast."
9. Franz Gilbert, "AI and the Reinvention of Human Recruiters," Talent Economy, January 2016.

10. Daniel Howden, "Interviews per Hire: Recruiting KPIs," Workable.com, April 2016.
11. Laszlo Bock, *Work Rules! Insights from Inside Google That Will Transform How You Live and Lead,* Hachette Book Group, 2015.
12. "Helping People See Better Through Strategic Talent Acquisition: A Recruitment Process Outsourcing Case Study," Korn Ferry Futurestep, Kornferry.com, 2016.

Chapter 9

1. Theresa Scherer, Jan Straub, Dan Schnyder, and Noemi Schaffner, "The Effects of Anonymity on Student Ratings of Teaching and Course Quality in Bachelor Degree Programs," Bern University of Applied Science, 2013.
2. Jason Laurtisen, "4 Reasons to Abandon Anonymity in Employee Surveys," Fistful of Talent, 2016.
3. Dana Wilkie, "Employee Engagement Surveys: Why Do Workers Distrust Them?," SHRM, 2017.
4. David Burkus, "Why Amazon Bought into Zappos's 'Pay to Quit' Policy," *Inc.,* 2016.
5. "The Smartest Thing Zappos HR Ever Did," Fistful of Talent, 2017.
6. Ibid.

Chapter 10

1. "2016–2017 HR Systems Survey," Sierra-Cedar.
2. "Raising the World-Class Bar in HR Through Digital Transformation," 2017 study, Hackett Group.
3. Deloitte's Global Human Capital Trends survey, 2017.
4. Dave Zielinski, "6 Tips for Finding the Right HRIS," SHRM, September 2016.
5. Dave Zielinski, "Artificial Intelligence Can Free HR Professionals to Focus on Strategy," SHRM, July 2017.
6. Interview with the head of U.S. recruiting at Ernst and Young.

Chapter 11

1. Ram Charan, Dennis Carey, and Michael Useem, *Boards That Lead: When to Take Charge, When to Partner, and When to Stay Out of the Way*, Harvard Business Review Press, 2013.
2. Ken Favaro, Per-Ola Karlsson, and Gary L. Neilson, "The $112 Billion CEO Succession Problem," *Strategy+Business*, no. 79, Summer 2015.
3. Dennis Carey, Melanie Kusin, and Jane Stevenson, "How Companies Can Avoid CEO Hiring Failure," *Fortune*, May 2012.
4. Nathan Vardi, "Citigroup's Succession Disaster," *Forbes*, October 2012.
5. Dennis Carey and John Keller, "How the Ford Board Recruited Alan Mulally," *Directors & Boards,* 2012.

6. Bryce Hoffman, "Here's Why Ford's Mark Fields Had to Go," *Forbes*, 2017.
7. William Boston, "Volkswagen Ousts CEO Matthias Müller, Promotes Herbert Diess to Top Role," *Wall Street Journal*, April 12, 2018.
8. Joann Lublin, "What's in Your Blind Spot?," *Wall Street Journal*, April 13, 2012.
9. Dennis Carey and Matt Smith, "How Companies Are Using Simulations, Competitions, and Analytics to Hire," *Harvard Business Review*, April 2016.
10. Susanne E. Blazek, James Lewis, Jeff Jones, and Evelyn J. Orr, "Develop and Select the Best CEOs," Korn Ferry Institute, 2018.

Chapter 12

1. Ilene Gochman, Stu Crandell, and R. J. Heckman, "Executive Outlook: The Talent Imperative at the Top," Korn Ferry Institute, 2015.
2. Katie Kuehner-Hebert, "Ready, Set, Divest!," *CFO* magazine, March 3, 2015.
3. Dana Mattioli and Dan Strumpf, "M&A Deal Activity on Pace for Record Year," *Wall Street Journal*, August 10, 2015.
4. Leadership Development Global Survey, Korn Ferry, 2015.
5. "It's Time to Blow Up HR and Build Something New. Here's How," *Harvard Business Review*, July/August 2015.
6. "The Conference Board CEO Challenge 2015: Creating Opportunity out of Adversity—Building Innovative, People-Driven Organizations," Conference Board, 2015.
7. Ram Charan, Dominic Barton, and Dennis Carey, *Talent Wins: The New Playbook for Putting People First*, Harvard Business Press, 2018.

INDEX

Page numbers followed by *f* indicate figures.

ABOUT THE AUTHOR

RJ Heckman, PhD, Vice Chairman at Korn Ferry, has worked in the talent management consulting and leadership development fields for 25 years. He consults with many of Korn Ferry's 7,000 clients, representing a large number of the world's top organizations. He has worked as an internal HR leader for two Fortune 50 companies, as CEO of a global leadership advisory firm, and served as an advisor and consultant to boards, CEOs, and CHROs of more than 100 Global 1000 companies.

A published author and sought-after speaker, Heckman is a frequent presenter at both professional and academic venues such as the Harvard Business School, INSEAD, New York University, Texas A&M University, the University of Southern California, the University of Minnesota, the Bombay Management Association, Conference Board, the Human Resources Planning Society, HR Technology Conference, and the Society for Industrial/Organizational Psychology.

Heckman's thought leadership has been published in the *Wall Street Journal*, *Financial Times*, *HR Executive Magazine*, *Chief Learning Officer Magazine*, and *Human Resource Management Review*, among others.

Dr. Heckman earned his bachelor's degree from the University of Wisconsin-Madison, and completed his graduate studies with a PhD in Industrial/Organizational Psychology from the University of Tulsa.